PRINCESS DIANA'S
Maternity Fashion and Nursery Handbook

PRINCESS DIANA'S
Maternity Fashion and Nursery Handbook

Sue James
FASHION EDITOR OF WOMAN'S OWN

Milánkovi a Janečkovi babička.

CRESCENT BOOKS
New York

Author's Acknowledgements
The author would like to express her gratitude to the following people,
without whose assistance this book could not have been written:
Phyllis Greene Morgan of *Dancercise*, for devising and demonstrating the
maternity exercises on pages 30-39, Belinda Banks for photographing them,
and Bridget Morley for drawing them.
Chris Welch for making up and providing detailed instructions for the
original dressmaking patterns given in chapter 4, and Jane Tyrrell
for the drawings to go with them.
David Hicks, Laura Ashley, Linda Beard, Designer's Guild and Mothercare
for their generous contributions of nursery designs, and Rosie Fisher of
Dragons and the Paul Press for allowing us to use material from their book
A Room To Grow Up In (Ebury Press 1984). All have been generous with
their time and advice.
Jan Vanvelden, and David Sassoon of Bellville Sassoon
for letting us use their original design sketches and for their invaluable
comments and advice.
Sally Muir and Joe Osborne of Warm and Wonderful for their picture sweater
design on page 112.
William Hollins for supplying Viyella fabrics, the European Commission
for the Promotion of Silk for supplying silk fabrics,
and Patons and Baldwins for supplying wool,
all for the patterns given in chapter 4.
Sarah Toynbee for her indefatigable research into facts and pictures.
Tim and Eileen Graham for their help and efficiency in providing us with their
invariably excellent photographs.
Finally, my husband, friends, the staff of *Woman's Own*, and all those others
in the fashion and publishing business who have been so generous with their
time and advice.

Planned and produced by Robert MacDonald Publishing
Designed by Bridget Morley
© Robert MacDonald Publishing, Sue James 1984
© in Dancercise and Aquacise, Phyllis Greene Morgan 1984
© in dressmaking patterns and designs, Sue James, 1984
First published in Great Britain by Orbis Publishing Limited
London 1984
Published in the United States 1984 by Crescent Books,
distributed by Crown Publishers, Inc.

Typeset by Wordsmith's Graphics, Street
Originated by Cromolito S.N.C., Milan
Printed by Proost, Belgium

Library of Congress Cataloging in Publication Data
James, Sue
        Princess Diana's Maternity Fashion and Nursery Handbook.

        1. Maternity Clothes.   2. Infants' Clothing
3. Nurseries – Equipment and Supplies.   4. Diana,
Princess of Wales, 1961 –   – Clothing. I. Title
TT547.J36 1984   646'.34   84-21480
ISBN 0-517-457806

h g f e d c b a

CONTENTS

Preface

This book not only celebrates the birth of a new member of the Royal Family – Prince Henry Charles Albert David, third in line to the throne and second son of the Prince and Princess of Wales – but marks the beginning of an era of modern-style Royal Family life. Much of this is due to the Princess, whose attitudes towards maternity and bringing up children are plainly very much in keeping with those of other modern mothers today. Both she and Prince Charles, obviously delighted with their young family, are determined to lead, as far as possible, a normal family life, and they are prepared to break with tradition to do so. Many people say that family life is under threat in the modern world. If so, the example of Britain's most famous family will surely help to resist it. They can be an inspiration to us all.

Writing this book has provided me with a wonderful excuse to take a look back at Royal children's dress through history, from Victorian times to the present day, and to see how it has always influenced the fashion of the times. Fortunately, today's Royal mothers dress their children in clothes that reflect modern tastes and the needs of modern living. Their practical and stylish approach has also inspired both the dress making and knitting patterns included in chapter four.

I have also been able to delve into the details of nursery life, including that of young Royals, past and present – and how interesting and intriguing it is. I am deeply grateful and delighted that such top interior designers as Laura Ashley, David Hicks, Designers Guild, Linda Beard and Dragons have been so generous in giving me their time, many original sketches and invaluable advice.

No book on maternity and nursery style would be complete without an in depth look at the Princess of Wales' fashion during her second pregnancy. Among other things, her obvious health (not many mothers appear in public looking as radiant as the Princess within twenty-four hours of the birth of their child) points up the importance of watching one's diet and of exercising regularly. This is never more important than during pregnancy, and one of the top experts in this field, Phyllis Greene Morgan of *Dancercise* has produced a set of exercises (or rather *Dancercises* and *Aquacises*) which I am sure would meet with the Princess's approval.

The Princess's natural style and flair never waver; they enhance and complement her decided taste and very positive views about clothes. She has lost none of the stylish elegance and naturalness of touch which distinguished her from the outset of her public career. She is indeed a wonderful ambassadress for British fashion. This is an opinion that is shared by many of her favourite dress designers, and I am delighted to have had the chance of working closely again with David Sassoon of Bellville Sassoon and Jan Vanvelden during the preparation of this book.

I hope that readers will enjoy a look into the fascinating background to the upbringing of Royal children, and that they will find the practical advice about how to give a regal touch to their own family lives helpful. I know that I have.

Sue James, September 1984

Maternity Fashion

The Princess of Wales, looking fit, happy and as elegant as ever,
emerges from St Mary's Paddington less than twenty-four hours
after the birth of Prince Harry.

For the Princess of Wales, motherhood was a turning point in her life. Since the birth of her first child, Prince William, she seems to have blossomed with a new stylishness and growing confidence. Her radiance has been apparent in every picture, and the Princess remains one of the most photographed women in the world – not only because she is the Princess of Wales and future Queen of England, but because she has a personality and a style that endear her to people from all walks of life. Diana, happily married and now with two children, has coped admirably with what must have been the major problem confronting her – the need to balance her public role as the Princess of Wales with her private role as wife and mother. In today's world, where many women have to balance their professional lives against their private ones, she sets a stimulating example. Few women, of course, are subjected to such intense scrutiny as the Princess, but even under the continuous spotlight of public attention she has grown more relaxed and confident over the past three years, and the pleasure and enjoyment that both she and Prince Charles get from married life have been obvious. The Royal Family occupy a unique place in British society; they are both a symbol and an example to the nation as a whole. Charles and Diana's secure and happy married life will be a source of satisfaction in the years to come, not just to the couple themselves, but to all of us.

Looking back over the past three years, one of the most obvious things that we all noticed immediately about Princess Diana was that she was different: unlike so many women in positions of public importance, she had *style*. And her style was one that could be, and was, copied by women all over the world. This influence in fashion was evident right from the beginning when, well before the wedding, 'Lady Di' frilly shirts flooded onto the high streets, and today it remains as strong as ever, whatever her critics might say. Although she has never been an innovator, Diana is obviously a woman who enjoys clothes. They interest her, and she has the looks, taste and flair to make the most of them. She has never regarded them as merely something to wear. It is this that marks her out from so many of her companions on the public stage. Like many other fashionable women, she has become more settled and mature in her style of dress. She now knows exactly what she likes and what she needs. There are fewer experiments and fewer outfits that are only likely to be worn once, but the calm confidence and the sheer stylishness are more in evidence than ever.

Nowhere was this more true than in her second pregnancy. Compared to the first, the Princess wore fewer different outfits and stuck mainly to the same style of dress throughout. Significantly, she did not rush straight into maternity outfits as soon the pregnancy was announced, but preferred to carry on wearing her normal clothes for the first few months while they were still comfortable and suited her. She could easily afford to, of course, because she maintained the slim model-like figure that she acquired after the birth of Prince William right up to – and through – her second pregnancy. Like many modern

A radiant picture of young motherhood; the Princess of Wales at London's Royal Opera House early in her second pregnancy.

mothers-to-be, Diana knows that there is no need to change your eating habits or to give up exercise because you are expecting a baby; in fact, she has stated publicly that she swims several lengths of a swimming pool each day during pregnancy. Today, doctors encourage women to keep fit and slim – where possible, of course – during this period of their lives. (See pages 30-39 for details of maternity exercises). Certainly Diana's slimness would have made it easier for her to incorporate her normal clothes, and many of the familiar 'Lady Di' details, into her maternity wardrobe. Perhaps another, less important, point is that most women cannot wait to get into maternity clothes when they are first pregnant; they are facing a new and exciting experience. However, possibly wiser the second time around, they realise that the earlier you move into maternity wear, the sooner you will be longing to wear slim-fitting clothes again. Nine months seems a short time at the beginning and a very long time at the end. Many women will have felt this, and possibly Diana did too.

Whatever the differences between them, the Princess's two pregnancies are linked by a major common factor – her sense of style. Far too many women sacrifice any thought of fashion during pregnancy to the need for easiness and comfort: but not the Princess of Wales. Diana has shown on both occasions that it is perfectly possible to combine dress sense with comfort (essential in any maternity clothes), without looking frumpish or boring in the least. An example is the suit in wool velour designed by Bellville Sassoon (facing page) which is both fashionable and slim-looking while remaining entirely suitable for pregnancy. The seven-eighths length coat is slightly fuller in shape, but to balance this, the skirt is slimmer. Worn with a blue and white striped crêpe-de-chine blouse, the overall effect is very flattering. Nor would the Princess go to the opposite extreme of wearing something too tight, which would look ugly and uncomfortable. The result is that she has looked both stylish and stunning – a tremendous compliment at any time, but one that any woman loves to hear when she is happily pregnant.

To some extent, the Princess has undoubtedly been helped by changing attitudes towards maternity wear, and towards pregnancy as a whole. Diana has never been one who liked wearing specialised maternity clothes – the type of billowing smocks that generations of women have been forced to wear because, until recently, there wasn't anything else. Some would say that the choice is still very poor, but one has only to look in the high-street windows to see that today's maternity clothes are much more varied and fashion conscious than those of the past. The Princess may not actually have caused these changes, but she has certainly had an influence, and she certainly takes full advantage of them. Changing attitudes towards pregnancy generally have also played a part in the Princess's style. Not long ago, women went into more or less total seclusion during pregnancy; today they often work until shortly before the birth, and there is now a genuine need for maternity clothes that are not so alien to everyday fashions.

Princess Diana is not the only member of the Royal Family to have benefitted from all this. Princess Anne, Princess Michael of Kent and the Duchess of Gloucester are other young Royal mothers who have escaped the restrictions imposed by convention on previous Royal

Changing styles in Royal pregnancy. Left: blue wool velour three-quarter length jacket and matching skirt, with toning blouse, designed by Bellville Sassoon and worn on arrival at Oslo airport for the Princes's solo visit to Norway in February 1984. Above: in contrast, the coat with fringed detail, also designed by Bellville Sassoon, which she wore during her first pregnancy on a visit to the Guildhall, Christmas 1981. The Princess's love of strong colours provides the link between these striking outfits.

Simple, tailored coats were a consistent choice during the Princess's second pregnancy. Above: an elegant navy overcoat, designed by Jan Vanvelden, demonstrating how flattering this line can be during the early stages of pregnancy. It was worn several times, on this occasion being greeted at Chester station in June 1984. Facing page: the style dubbed by the press as 'Diana's teddy boy look'. The coat is in one of the Princess's favourite styles.

generations. When the Queen Mother was expecting Princess Elizabeth, it seemed that the first the world knew about it was when the child was born. It was said that Queen Victoria was quite shocked that Princess Alexandra, the wife of Prince Edward, was still carrying on an active social life whilst pregnant, even though her activities were private rather than public. Queen Victoria herself hated being pregnant (despite the fact that she managed it so often) and in those days Royal pregnancies were never announced. It is thus in a much more relaxed and informal atmosphere that today's Royal Family goes through pregnancy; plainly this new approach suits Princess Diana as much as it pleases her army of admirers.

Easier things may be, but the problems of dressing through pregnancy stay the same – in fact they may be even more acute now that higher standards have become the norm. Special occasions demand that you dress smartly, pregnancy notwithstanding and there is always the danger of overdoing it or of splashing out on an outfit that you can never wear again during your pregnancy. And while some people believe that special maternity clothes can be worn again afterwards with only slight adjustments, there are plenty of others who don't, and they are probably right. Well made maternity clothes are cut to suit a pregnant shape, and simply taking in a bit here and there will seldom make them look right. Immediately after the birth, such clothes might come in useful; but once you have regained your shape and your sanity they tend to be dismissed and packed away. This does not, of course, rule out the reverse idea of wearing your ordinary clothes during pregnancy for as long as you can. As Diana has shown, this is entirely practical and sensible.

The Princess has a very positive attitude to maternity clothes – as she does to her normal clothes. Her wardrobe provides her with the casual, smart and evening outfits that her lifestyle demands. She does, of course, have more outfits than would most women during their pregnancies, but no more than her official duties as Princess of Wales require. She must anyway maintain a certain level of dressing, and it has never been Diana's style to wear unattractive clothes that lack elegance. Instead, she indulges her taste for clothes that are simple and easy. She sticks to pretty colours that enhance her natural colouring and skin tones, and chooses cool, lightweight fabrics, especially for the summer months, such as silk, lightweight wools and crêpe de chine and cotton. Natural fibres do let the body breathe better, which makes them comfortable during pregnancy when you tend to get easily overheated.

Looking at the clothes worn by the Princess of Wales since her first pregnancy, there is no doubt that she has worked out several styles which she both likes and which suit her. Her coats, for example, are very simple and follow through the tailored, almost mannish, overcoat style that was fashionable during the winter of 1983/1984. The navy single-breasted wool crêpe coat that was designed for her by Jan Vanvelden had a strong classic tailored look and, for practical reasons, had front and shoulder tucks as extra detail. Underneath it, the Princess wore a favourite simple white winged-collar shirt, first seen on the Royal tour of Canada in 1983. The Princess also appeared several times in the herringbone coat with a velvet collar, which the press nicknamed 'Diana's teddy boy look' (see facing page), demon-

The Princess is not afraid of wearing the same dress more than once. This must be one of her best-loved styles. Both these dresses were designed by the Chelsea Design Company, identical except for the fabric, and have been worn for both formal and informal occasions. Above left: at the wedding of ex-flatmate Carolyn Pride in 1981. Above right: worn casually to watch Charles play polo in June 1984. Right: on a more formal occasion, the official photo-call for Prince William's second birthday, also in June 1984.

strating the ease with which she was able to wear items from her normal wardrobe during the first few months of her pregnancy.

If coats are the problem in winter, then dresses and suits can be equally difficult in summer – particularly if, like Diana's, your baby is expected towards the end of the summer months. In both her pregnancies, Diana has adopted a favourite style in dresses. During the first, it was a spotted dress with front tie which she wore in several fabrics and colours. She wore one version of this when she left hospital after the birth of Prince William. Similarly, during the second pregnancy, some equally firm favourites emerged (see following pages), all reflecting the Princess's positive approach to her clothes. This practice of choosing a style that you like, and that is suitable and practical, and then sticking to it, is something that many stylish dressers follow. Instead of switching between several different looks, they tailor their clothes to two or three types of outfit that they can wear for many different types of occasion. These are, in fact, 'investment' clothes – outfits that you might have bought initially for a special occasion (and which aren't necessarily expensive) but which can then be worn for a variety of occasions, sometimes casual and sometimes smart.

The Princess of Wales has definitely learnt the art of investment dressing, and although it would be easy, and she could no doubt afford, to have a different dress for every occasion, this is not Diana's style. She knows that clothes should fit in with your lifestyle and work for you. Take, for instance, the drop-waist dress (see facing page) designed by the Chelsea Design Company. It shows all the details that are in keeping with Diana's style of dress. It has a simple drop waist, fairly loose fitting, in silk, with a sailor collar with narrow lapels and front tie. She first wore it to the wedding of her ex-flatmate Carolyn Pride in 1981, and it has reappeared on numerous occasions since. It is a dress that the Princess obviously feels comfortable in, and she knows that it is suitable for different places at different times – not just for Wimbledon or polo matches, but also, no doubt because it is so flattering as well as comfortable, for the official photographic session for Prince William's second birthday. She even has another dress in the same style but in a different fabric and another colour – soft blue.

For Princess Diana, this way of dressing certainly serves as a rebuke to those critics who complain about the size of her wardrobe and its cost; but, for any woman, it is obviously a sensible and practical approach to take. It is not always so easy of course. You may be one of those women whose size alters too much and too rapidly for you to be able to contemplate wearing your ordinary clothes during pregnancy, however loose they may be. But the same principles can easily be applied to the maternity clothes you are going to need. And when you are shopping for maternity clothes during the early months of pregnancy, it is well worth pausing for thought and checking to see whether there are non-maternity styles that you like that could be adapted later on to suit your altered shape; these at least can be put back to their original shape and worn after the baby is born. It is important to have at least one versatile outfit during pregnancy, one that you can wear for both casual and smart occasions, since it can solve many of the headaches about what to wear and when. The dress pattern given on page 132 is an example of the sort of style that will

The Princess, visiting the Albany Community Project in Deptford in May 1984, meets London's Pearly King (dressed in traditional if unorthodox fashion) and his family. Her outfit includes the large zig-zag collar that has become a trademark of hers as well as of the designer, Jan Vanvelden.

see you through your pregnancy without too many problems of whether you are over- or under-dressed.

Another investment look from Diana's maternity wardrobe is the two-piece outfit. Separates can be unflattering if you get very big in pregnancy and they may not be quite smart enough for a special occasion, but this simple shirt-style top with a matching soft pleated skirt can solve both problems. Designed by Jan Vanvelden, this patterned two-piece in 'Liberty' wool has the large zig-zag collar that has become a trademark not just of the designer but of the Princess as well. Details around the collar – wing or sailor collar, cravat, or small ruffles and bows – are a common feature of Princess Diana's outfits and are a clever way of taking the emphasis away from the tummy during pregnancy. Another example, also designed by Jan Vanvelden, was the soft blue jacket and dress that she wore for the Trooping of the Colour ceremony in 1984. The white sailor collar worn with it provided a striking 'Diana' detail. The simple two-piece style was seen again when Diana attended Ascot in June 1984. Six months pregnant, she wore a two-piece in coral silk crêpe de chine jacquard, again designed by Jan Vanvelden, who says that this look is perfect for maternity because it is both feminine and elegant. "It's a time when women want to look as they feel – very feminine. And it's important that they feel comfortable and wear clothes that suit them." His two-piece outfit reflects this philosophy. The tunic shirt top has a wing collar and matching cravat. Again, he uses the tucks that form soft pleats to give ease and movement in the shirt top, and the skirt is softly pleated so that it is slimmer without being restricting. (See overleaf for the original designs for these two outfits.)

This type of outfit is marvellous if you want to get maximum mileage out of your clothes. Wear the shirt-style top with a plain skirt, or under a pinafore dress (which is always a good investment buy). The skirt can be worn with a plain shirt or sweater. Always make sure, when you wear the two halves of a specific outfit separately, that you team them with something that is suitable not only in style but in fabric as well. For instance, a soft pleated skirt in silk would not look good with a thick heavy knitted sweater, but would go well with a soft lacy one. And a shirt in a delicate fabric like silk would team well with anything from wool to corduroy or even denim, but not with a sweat-style fabric.

Of course, an inexpensive way of improvising a two-piece outfit from your existing wardrobe is to take a large tunic top or a big shirt (like a man's shirt), ideally shaped to double up as a maternity top, and then make or buy a maternity skirt to wear with it. You will find that a collarless large white or fine-striped man's shirt looks great with a simple skirt – in white for summer and black for winter – and smart too. A tunic and skirt pattern in this style is given on page 138.

The Princess has always paid great attention to detail, particularly to accessories, which can make or break even the simplest outfit. She has decided tastes in hats – required wearing for Royal ladies at official engagements. One of her favourites is the small veiled style of hat designed by John Boyd, which is reported to be particularly liked by Prince Charles as well. Otherwise, she has always kept her accessories to a minimum, preferring to keep to one single, distinctive piece of jewellery, such as the much favoured twist pearl rope choker or simple

Hats have always been a distinctive part of Diana's wardrobe, and the smaller veiled or feathered styles have remained firm favourites right up to the present. Top left: hat and veil at Chester in June 1984, designed by John Boyd. Top right: small pill-box style hat, again designed by John Boyd, worn for a visit to the Sue Ryder Home in Cheltenham in March 1984. Below: a wider-brimmed style, designed by Frederick Fox, as the Princess drives away in her new Ford Escort Cabriolet on a sunny day at Smith's Lawn in June 1984.

"When women are pregnant, I think they want to look and feel feminine" says Jan Vanvelden, who designed this silk crêpe de chine two-piece suit for the Princess during her second pregnancy. He has certainly fulfilled his intentions here, with an outfit that manages to be very feminine without being at all fanciful. The suit has an easy shirt-style tunic with matching cravat and soft skirt. The colour follows through the Princess's preference for soft pastels for summer maternity wear, and the fabric, being silk, is cool and very light. Jan Vanvelden is one of the few of the Princess's designers to present a whole range of specialist maternity wear (which can be seen at Great Expectations in London's Fulham Road). He feels that maternity colours should not be complicated and that these more elegant clothes are preferable to sporty separates.

The Princess has shown her approval of this particular outfit by wearing it on several occasions, including Ascot. Here, she wears a hat to tone with the outfit, but this time a broad-brimmed one rather than a pillbox style.

A rhapsody in blue. Diana first wore this dress and jacket designed, like the outfit on the opposite page, by Jan Vanvelden for the Trooping of the Colour ceremony in June 1984 and again a bit later in the month when she visited Odstock Hospital near Salisbury. This outfit, from Jan Vanvelden's spring/summer range for 1984, was carefully adapted for the Princess. "It is a very simple outfit that can be worn for many different occasions", Jan tells us. The dress has a tuck front that falls into loose pleats just below the waist, short sleeves and a detatchable sailor-style collar. The jacket has a simple round neck and is edge to edge. Both are made in wool crêpe. Following through the pale blue theme, Diana chose a small veiled hat to match, and added just a twisted pearl choker and matching earrings for jewellery. As usual, she kept the outfit very simple.

19

Even in maternity clothes and at her most casual, Diana never loses her fashion flair. As in her first pregnancy, the Princess often looked at her most attractive and most appealing when 'off duty', as in these cropped trousers and over-sized sweater at a weekend polo match.

pearl earrings. As Diana well knows, too much jewellery, or indeed the wrong combination of materials such as plastic and pearls, can end up looking just a mess.

As far as shoes are concerned, the Princess has remained consistently faithful to variations on her favourite low pumps, often in a two-tone colourway, such as navy and white, and sometimes with a peep toe or wedge or a bow trim. Most of them are, in fact, still made by W.H.Rayne, a company which has been supplying shoes to the Royal Family for many years. Tights can be extremely uncomfortable both when you are pregnant and when it is hot. Diana either makes a feature of them by wearing them in colours that tone with or complement a colour in her outfit (see page 11), or, in high summer, she goes bare legged at every possible opportunity. Finally, the Princess does not like large cumbersome handbags for smart occasions, and sticks to a neat clutch bag or small shoulder bag. These small purse-shaped bags on a strap can look very good worn across the body when you are pregnant, and they save you the trouble of actually holding a bag. All these extras are well worth attention. The rules of good dress sense apply just as much during pregnancy as at any other time. Indeed, as your shape becomes more awkward, so it becomes even more important to choose the right accessories for your outfit.

Casual Clothes

Diana's approach to her casual clothes – her off-duty looks – differs very little from her approach to the smart outfits which make up her 'official' wardrobe. She chooses clothes that are both fashionable and comfortable, keeping the style very relaxed and often relying on one or two favourite looks. For many women, looking at the Princess's wardrobe, these casual clothes represent very much the sort of things they would like to wear themselves every day. It may well be that Diana's casual clothes are actually a truer reflection of her personality than her more formal wear – a younger, less conventional Princess seems to emerge. Whatever the case, there is no doubt that Diana enjoys clothes as much during pregnancy as she does the rest of the time; her sense of style is undiminished, and her example is fun to follow.

Like many young mothers-to-be, Diana has found that there are simple and easy-to-wear dresses that can look good whatever the occasion. During her recent pregnancy, she has shown a particular liking for one particular style, a versatile drop-waist dress which she has in two different colourways, and which she has worn on several occasions. A pattern for a dress in this style is given on page 141. This is exactly the sort of outfit that you could wear to the office, for a lunch or to a wedding. It would be hard to think of a better investment. During her first pregnancy, one of Diana's most appealing outfits was the 'Australian' fun picture sweater by Jenny Kee, featuring a Koala bear, worn with a pair of red cords (hardly conventional maternity wear, but Diana has never minded breaking the rules). The second time around, she chose for summer wear a pair of cropped pants and long-line sweater. It is interesting to see the extent to which the specialised maternity shops, Mothercare among them, are now pro-

Lightweight summer jackets are essential in the British climate, and if sufficiently loose-fitting, they don't have to be specialist maternity wear. Here she wears a Jasper Conran design, bought well before her first pregnancy.

ducing tunics, trackpants and jumpsuits, often in cotton sweatshirt fabric and in a variety of different colours. Clothes like these do not necessarily have to be made specially for maternity. If you look around the high street shops and stores (Harrods, Benetton and Harvey Nichols for example) you may well find ordinary clothes in these styles that you can wear while pregnant. But take care. Remember that you will grow over the months, and it is not every figure that can take such clothes anyway. Many women forget that it is not just the front view that counts, but the back view as well. In other words, these more 'sporty' clothes can work well, but only if they suit you and your figure. The Princess kept comparatively slim throughout both her pregnancies, and didn't have too many problems. She also took very good care that nothing fitted too tightly. Dressing in anything too tight during pregnancy makes the clothes look unsightly and you even larger. One of the golden rules of dressing well, whether you are pregnant or not, is never buy clothes that are too small.

A more versatile style of casual trouser wear, which is often easier to suit to awkward figure shapes and sizes, is the maternity-style dungarees. These can look very attractive worn with a t-shirt or a man's shirt. Don't make the mistake of wearing your dungarees big and baggy and then teaming them with a tight or skimpy fitting sweater or shirt underneath. This can look very unflattering. An exclusive pattern for a pair of maternity dungarees which you can make for yourself is given on page 135.

Jackets and top coats can be a problem during pregnancy. Diana chose a very simple coat style for the early months of her pregnancy (see page 12). But that was in winter, and it is really in the summer months, particularly in England where the sun can't be relied upon to shine, that the problems occur. Summer evenings can be chilly, and it is then that you need a versatile, lightweight jacket that will go with most of your clothes. A good example is the one that Princess Diana has worn – a very lightweight, almost cardigan-style, jacket which works well with dresses as well as with pants and skirts. Diana did not buy this specially for her pregnancy – in fact she had it several seasons ago – but, like many other women, she has found that once you have a good basic wardrobe, then you can often wear many of the outfits time and time again. This particular jacket was designed by Jasper Conran, and was part of his collection for Autumn 1981.

When choosing a jacket, make sure that you consider beforehand all the different outfits you might be wearing it with. This type of garment can, of course, be worn after pregnancy, but if you are planning to make much use of it while you are pregnant, it is probably better to stick to neutral colours like cream, grey and black. The style of the jacket should be fairly easy so that it will fit with either smart or casual clothes. If you buy anything too distinctive, such as a highly tailored blazer or a sporty anorak, you may well find that you can only wear it with clothes of a similar type.

A way of avoiding all these problems would be to buy a serap or a large thro-over shawl coat. These will not only suit all figures, but most styles of clothes as well. One made in jersey or fine wool would be suitable for both autumn/winter and spring/summer. In colder weather you can wear a jacket or heavy cardigan underneath to give an extra layer for warmth.

The Princess of Wales, less than a month before the birth of Prince Harry, looks casual and fresh in a Laura Ashley pinafore dress, as she arrives at Aberdeen airport for a holiday at Balmoral. The blouse has the distinctive 'Diana style' collar.

Evening Wear

If there is one aspect of the Princess of Wales' fashion that has consistently delighted and amazed her audience, and won their wholehearted applause, it is her evening wear. It was in an evening gown – a black strapless dress designed by David and Elizabeth Emanuel – that she first hit the fashion headlines when she attended her first official function, as Lady Diana Spencer, in March 1981; and she has not disappointed us since. Princess Diana brought glamour back to evening wear, with a sparkling array of fairy-tale ballgowns and slim slinky evening dresses. Manufacturers the world over have copied her styles and designs. And although the Princess, like everyone else, wears the same outfits for several different occasions, she has remained entirely unpredictable, always liable to break with convention – even conventions of her own making – and appear in something completely unexpected. She could have found no more effective way of silencing her critics in Australia than by wearing the one-shoulder evening dress that managed to be enormously glamorous and full of sex-appeal. Diana's evening wear is the clearest possible statement that here is a Princess who is not going to be bound by staid conventions and who is determined to enjoy her gifts of charm and beauty to the full.

The Princess has lost none of her touch during her latest pregnancy. In March 1984, she and Prince Charles attended a Genesis concert at the National Exhibition Centre in Birmingham. Diana, to everyone's surprise, wore an entirely unorthodox tuxedo suit. Not only was this in complete contrast to what was expected of a Princess, but she was three months pregnant at the time. The masculine-style cream tuxedo jacket with wing-collar shirt and simple black pants was designed by Margaret Howell. The outfit was extremely elegant and very stylish and it stole the show.

Of course, tuxedos and slinky evening dresses are not always appropriate evening wear for the Princess of Wales. And it is for these rather more conventional or formal occasions that Diana brings out her beautiful traditional evening gowns. A number of these have been in evidence during both her pregnancies, though not always designed for specific occasions, nor even necessarily for maternity. The beautiful 'Empire style' white georgette evening dress with silver glitter spray, designed by Bellville Sassoon and worn in May 1984 to Burlington House for a formal dinner at the Royal Academy of Arts, was in fact made for her first pregnancy, although it was very much in keeping with her style during her second. The dress has a regency feel to it, with a high waistline, tiered sleeves and deep buttoning cuffs. David Sassoon has his own views about the problems of dressing during pregnancy. "It's a mistake to combine too many details; the simpler the style, the more flattering it is."

A ballgown with a high waist is an effective way of disguising a bigger tummy. However, a soft drape style can be equally effective. The Princess wore a luxurious wrap-over evening dress of this kind to the première of *Indiana Jones and the Temple of Doom* in June 1984. Designed by the Chelsea Design Company, the dress had a definite 1920s feel to it. It was made in rich silk satin and had a shawl collar neckline, a draped drop waist and a full skirt that fell into folds. The

Facing page: the Princess's ability to surprise has remained undiminished. At the Genesis concert in Birmingham in March 1984, she abandoned ballgowns and tiaras in favour of a fashionable tuxedo suit. Again, at the première of Indiana Jones and the Temple of Doom *(overleaf, left), she breaks with tradition by wearing a drop-waist, '20s style evening dress, designed by the Chelsea Design Company. However, a more conventional style was clearly in order for the annual dinner of the Royal Academy of Arts at Burlington House in May 1984 (overleaf, right). This 'empire' style ballgown, designed by Bellville Sassoon, was in fact made for her first pregnancy and has been worn on several occasions.*

design is clever as well as appealing, and demonstrates that it is quite possible for a drop-waist style to soften the contours of the bulge rather than enhancing them. Again, although it was a new look for Diana, it fitted well with her continuously stylish dressing throughout her second pregnancy.

Buying an evening gown is an expensive business and you may not want to splash out on special maternity clothes for evening wear if you can't wear them later on. As the Princess has shown, there are a number of styles that can work as well for the pregnant figure as for the normal one. The basic rule is to keep the style of dress very simple, and to choose a beautiful fabric that moves and isn't too stiff. Add extra luxury and dazzle by going for a rich fabric that has some glitter or, perhaps, beading, but avoid anything excessive in fabric, colour or design. Choose any colour that really suits you, although black, cream, silver or red are the classics which will not date so quickly. Don't go overboard in your choice of accessories; if you dress in fairly luxurious fabrics, there is no need to add lots of extra sparkle with masses of real or fake jewellery. Stick to one big piece, like distinctive earrings or a bracelet, rather than a lot of tiny chains and so on. If you do have to buy a special maternity-style evening outfit, perhaps because of a very important occasion late on in your pregnancy, you should stick to a very simple plain dress in one of the classic colours. Here, you will need to add extra colour and interest with your accessories, so you can make rather more of your jewellery – striking earrings and a bracelet, for example, in matching red rhinestones. The overall effect should be that the different parts of your outfit all work together, rather than seeming to be a mixture of different styles.

Most women can manage without special maternity evening gowns. However, there comes a stage fairly late on in pregnancy when it can be difficult to know what to wear for a special evening occasion. These are the times when you are feeling heavy and a little awkward, but you have been asked out to dinner or to the theatre and not only want to look good, but stylish and elegant as well. This is when you need a dress that is a little too special for everyday wear, but not as dressy as formal evening wear; something in which you will feel comfortable but not overdressed. The answer is a loose fitting dress, not too full, and again very simple in style, relying on the fabric to make it look stunning. A pattern for a dress of the sort, which you can make for yourself, is given on page 141. You could wear it for a party or for dinner out both in winter and in summer. It is a style of dress that is extremely comfortable, particularly if you are eating a fairly large meal, or sitting down for long periods of time. The Princess herself wore something very similar to this at the Neil Diamond concert in July 1984. The dress was made of sparkling jersey and designed by Jasper Conran, who understands the problems of dressing in pregnancy. "If a woman feels awkward and unattractive, then she needs to wear a dress or outfit that makes her feel good, and special. Pay attention to fabric and styling; both are important. Go for simple dressing with no frills, tucks or flounces. Keep it as streamlined as possible." Certainly, this particular dress set off perfectly the health, charm and happiness that seemed to accompany the Princess throughout the days of both her pregnancies, and which will no doubt continue to accompany her through those still to come.

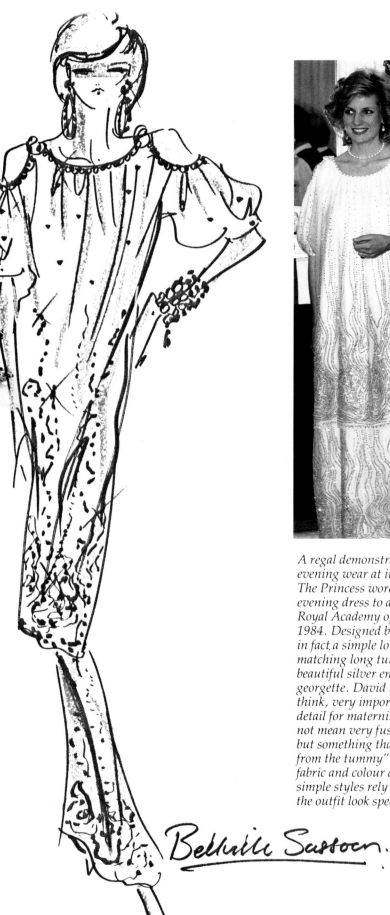

A regal demonstration of maternity evening wear at its best and most elegant. The Princess wore this long, slim-looking evening dress to a formal dinner at the Royal Academy of Arts on the 14th May, 1984. Designed by Bellville Sassoon, it is in fact a simple long sheath dress with a matching long tunic over the top, made in beautiful silver encrusted white silk georgette. David Sassoon tells us "It is, I think, very important to have neckline detail for maternity wear. By this, I do not mean very fussy necklines or collars, but something that distracts attention from the tummy". He also knows that fabric and colour are both important, as simple styles rely heavily on these to make the outfit look special.

Dancercise

If there is any time in your life when you need to be fit and healthy, it is during pregnancy. Dance as an exercise is remarkably effective and thorough, giving immediate results that last a lifetime. Dance itself brings pleasure and release from the hurly-burly of everyday life.

Phyllis Greene Morgan, who devised the special maternity exercises on the following pages, as well as writing the text and captions for them, has been evolving *Dancercise* for more than twelve years – a system dedicated to the proposition that all the world should have a chance to dance and the bodies to show for it. As Phyllis Greene Morgan writes:

"You may snicker from behind your ballooning belly, but I must tell you that the most memorable compliment I ever received as a woman was when I was burstingly pregnant: "How gloriously fruitful you look" he murmured. And so you should feel – fruitful, glorious and glowing with life...

...Well not all the time, perhaps. But in your state, you will feel better about your body, not to mention self and psyche, if you will just turn on some music and get up and dance.

Dance works so well as an exercise because it harmonises with the natural need for beauty. Your aesthetic self – and everyone has one – rejects ugly, unbecoming, movements – and boring ones. Dance gives you something to accomplish beyond the exercise itself – and it is a superb and thorough workout.

At Dancercise, bodies are regarded as person, not thing. Therefore, our exercises are designed to enhance and stimulate – rather than chop and change – whether our students are 'fat', 'thin', pregnant or post partem.

If you have never exercised before, or not regularly, go easy. For reassurance, show these pages to your doctor. In normal cases, however, there is not much you can do to stop the course of nature; witness the ladies of old who hurled themselves off kitchen tables to no avail.

Just use common sense. If you have a bump, you won't be very comfortable rolling on it. Don't stretch too mightily and avoid jumping. There is no reason why you cannot – and should not – exercise gently throughout your pregnancy. We have rolled many a woman from Dancercise to the delivery room. And though I admit it was an act of bravado, I taught a class while I was in labour.

Although there are many other factors involved, the better toned your muscles are, the better chance you have to give birth efficiently and enjoyably and to recover your shape swiftly afterwards.

Another advantage of starting systematic exercise before the Day is that you know there is salvation and a way back to the old figure beyond it.

I created these exercises to give you 1. suppleness of muscle and mobility of joint – so you feel like a gazelle rather than a hippo and so you can give birth gracefully in any position; 2. relief from anatomical and inevitable strain; and 3. a sense of beauty, so you feel elegant, sensual and feminine.

I hope you will enjoy them."

Phyllis Greene Morgan, 1984

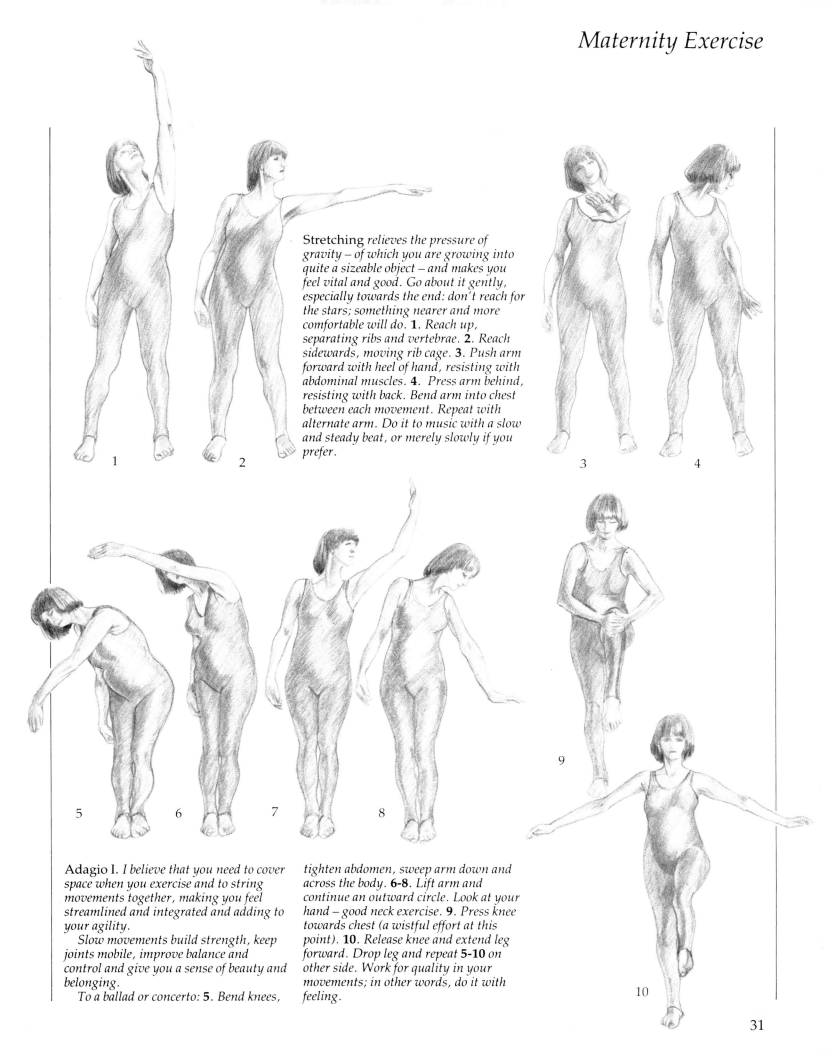

Stretching *relieves the pressure of gravity – of which you are growing into quite a sizeable object – and makes you feel vital and good. Go about it gently, especially towards the end: don't reach for the stars; something nearer and more comfortable will do.* **1.** *Reach up, separating ribs and vertebrae.* **2.** *Reach sidewards, moving rib cage.* **3.** *Push arm forward with heel of hand, resisting with abdominal muscles.* **4.** *Press arm behind, resisting with back. Bend arm into chest between each movement. Repeat with alternate arm. Do it to music with a slow and steady beat, or merely slowly if you prefer.*

Adagio I. *I believe that you need to cover space when you exercise and to string movements together, making you feel streamlined and integrated and adding to your agility.*

Slow movements build strength, keep joints mobile, improve balance and control and give you a sense of beauty and belonging.

To a ballad or concerto: **5.** *Bend knees,* tighten abdomen, sweep arm down and across the body. **6-8.** *Lift arm and continue an outward circle. Look at your hand – good neck exercise.* **9.** *Press knee towards chest (a wistful effort at this point).* **10.** *Release knee and extend leg forward. Drop leg and repeat* **5-10** *on other side. Work for quality in your movements; in other words, do it with feeling.*

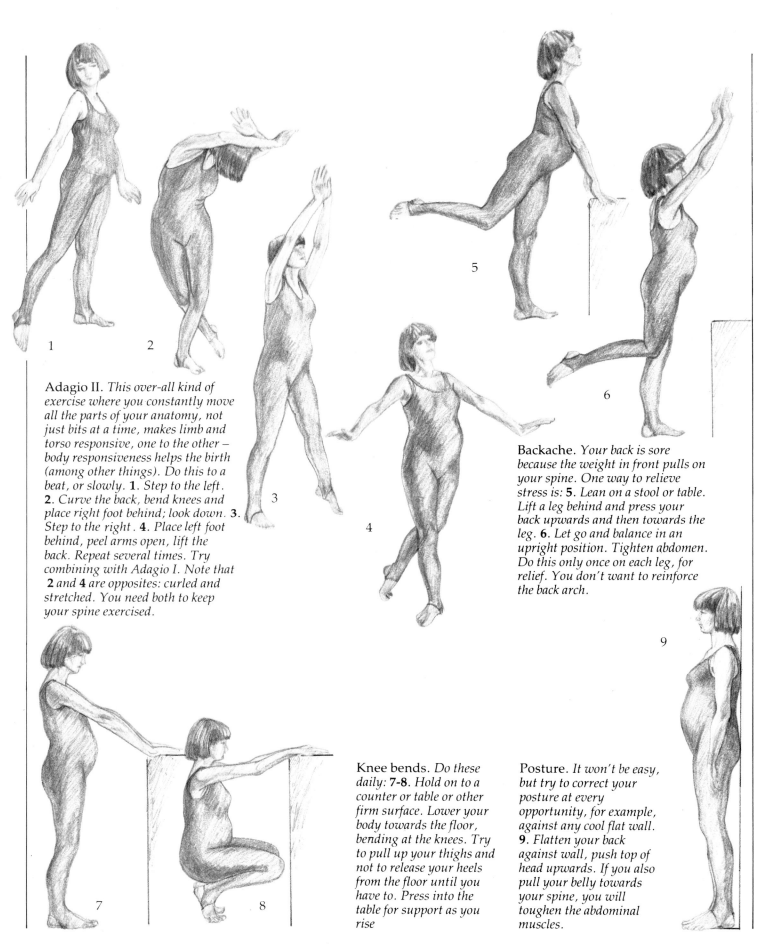

Adagio II. *This over-all kind of exercise where you constantly move all the parts of your anatomy, not just bits at a time, makes limb and torso responsive, one to the other – body responsiveness helps the birth (among other things). Do this to a beat, or slowly.* **1***. Step to the left.* **2***. Curve the back, bend knees and place right foot behind; look down.* **3***. Step to the right .* **4***. Place left foot behind, peel arms open, lift the back. Repeat several times. Try combining with Adagio I. Note that* **2** *and* **4** *are opposites: curled and stretched. You need both to keep your spine exercised.*

Backache. *Your back is sore because the weight in front pulls on your spine. One way to relieve stress is:* **5***. Lean on a stool or table. Lift a leg behind and press your back upwards and then towards the leg.* **6***. Let go and balance in an upright position. Tighten abdomen. Do this only once on each leg, for relief. You don't want to reinforce the back arch.*

Knee bends. *Do these daily:* **7-8***. Hold on to a counter or table or other firm surface. Lower your body towards the floor, bending at the knees. Try to pull up your thighs and not to release your heels from the floor until you have to. Press into the table for support as you rise*

Posture. *It won't be easy, but try to correct your posture at every opportunity, for example, against any cool flat wall.* **9***. Flatten your back against wall, push top of head upwards. If you also pull your belly towards your spine, you will toughen the abdominal muscles.*

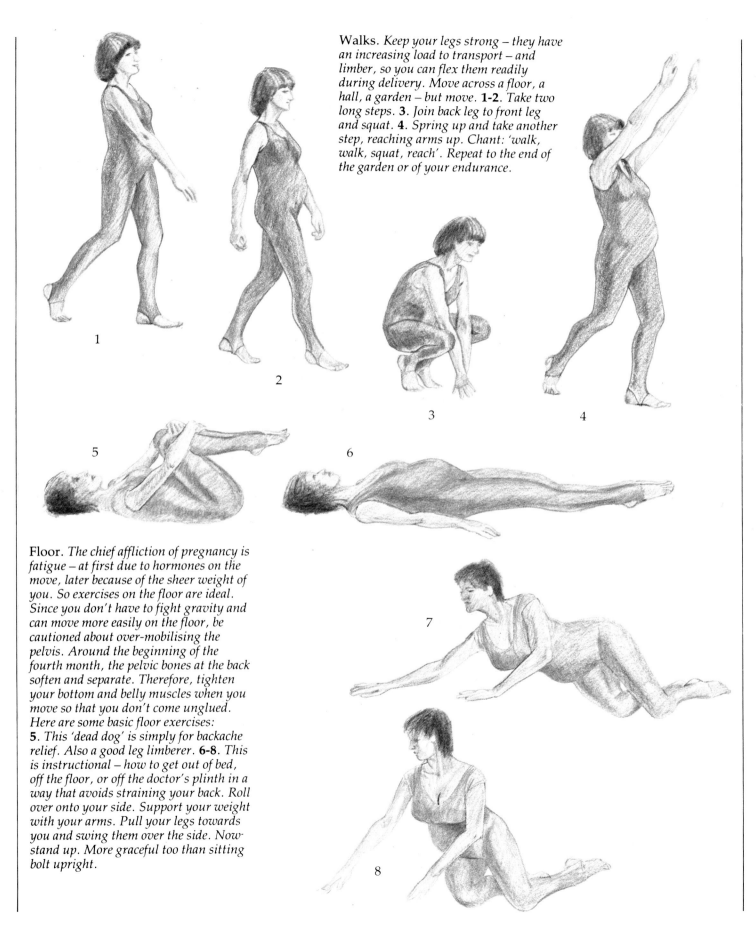

Walks. *Keep your legs strong – they have an increasing load to transport – and limber, so you can flex them readily during delivery. Move across a floor, a hall, a garden – but move.* **1-2.** *Take two long steps.* **3.** *Join back leg to front leg and squat.* **4.** *Spring up and take another step, reaching arms up. Chant: 'walk, walk, squat, reach'. Repeat to the end of the garden or of your endurance.*

1

2

3

4

5

6

7

8

Floor. *The chief affliction of pregnancy is fatigue – at first due to hormones on the move, later because of the sheer weight of you. So exercises on the floor are ideal. Since you don't have to fight gravity and can move more easily on the floor, be cautioned about over-mobilising the pelvis. Around the beginning of the fourth month, the pelvic bones at the back soften and separate. Therefore, tighten your bottom and belly muscles when you move so that you don't come unglued. Here are some basic floor exercises:* **5.** *This 'dead dog' is simply for backache relief. Also a good leg limberer.* **6-8.** *This is instructional – how to get out of bed, off the floor, or off the doctor's plinth in a way that avoids straining your back. Roll over onto your side. Support your weight with your arms. Pull your legs towards you and swing them over the side. Now stand up. More graceful too than sitting bolt upright.*

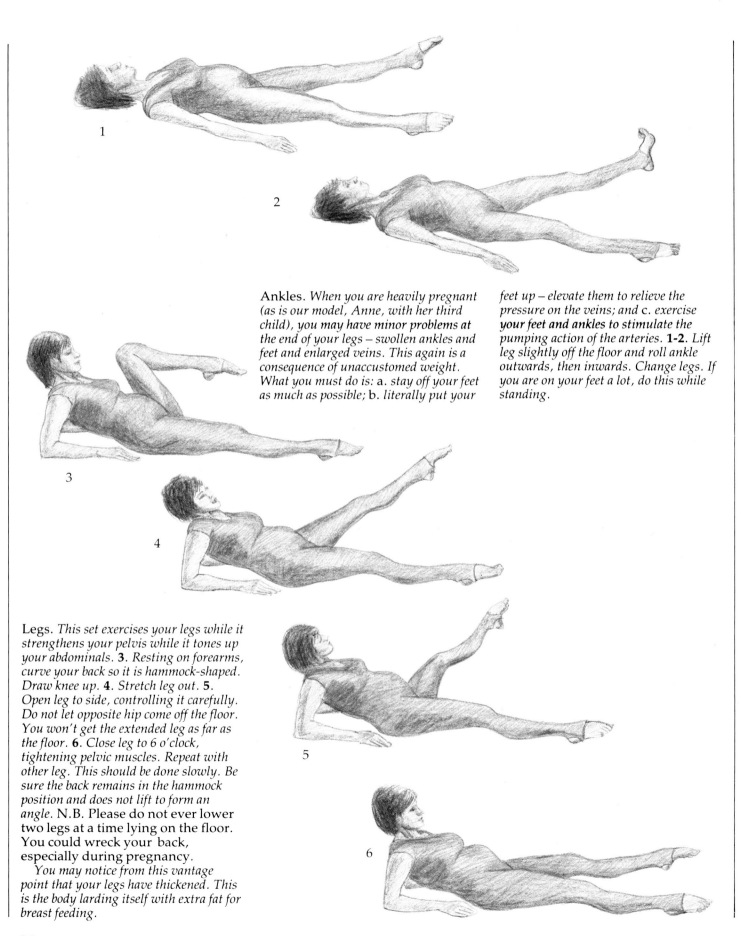

Ankles. *When you are heavily pregnant (as is our model, Anne, with her third child), you may have minor problems at the end of your legs – swollen ankles and feet and enlarged veins. This again is a consequence of unaccustomed weight. What you must do is:* a. *stay off your feet as much as possible;* b. *literally put your feet up – elevate them to relieve the pressure on the veins; and* c. *exercise* **your feet and ankles** *to stimulate the pumping action of the arteries.* **1-2.** *Lift leg slightly off the floor and roll ankle outwards, then inwards. Change legs. If you are on your feet a lot, do this while standing.*

Legs. *This set exercises your legs while it strengthens your pelvis while it tones up your abdominals.* **3.** *Resting on forearms, curve your back so it is hammock-shaped. Draw knee up.* **4.** *Stretch leg out.* **5.** *Open leg to side, controlling it carefully. Do not let opposite hip come off the floor. You won't get the extended leg as far as the floor.* **6.** *Close leg to 6 o'clock, tightening pelvic muscles. Repeat with other leg. This should be done slowly. Be sure the back remains in the hammock position and does not lift to form an angle.* N.B. Please do not ever lower two legs at a time lying on the floor. You could wreck your back, especially during pregnancy.

You may notice from this vantage point that your legs have thickened. This is the body larding itself with extra fat for breast feeding.

Knees diamond shaped. 1. *Use this position to limber your legs for birth. You can also relieve back pain or tension by pulling towards your ankles with a straight back. Don't bounce: do it deliberately.*

Kenwood. *This leg exercise also works the hips and wrings the spine a bit, which is good for it.* **2.** *Sit with legs apart (only as far as is not uncomfortable).* **3.** *Turn left knee in.* **4.** *Stretch left leg out.* **5.** *Bend left knee again.* **6.** *Open left knee to the left.* **7.** *Stretch it out to the left. Repeat with the other leg. Once you have got it, try to join up the movements so they are like plaiting with your legs.*

Dancercise and Aquacise *are protected trade names, registered by Phyllis Greene Morgan and may not be used by anyone else to describe their classes either generally or particularly.*

Floor Adagio. *Exercise should make you feel better in yourself and about yourself. It won't work unless you enjoy it – and that is a scientific fact. Moving harmoniously is enjoyable. So is mastering movements, like the ones in this floor adagio. Learn the movements separately. Then do them in a continuous, sinuous chain. Follow our model as if she were beside you, not facing you. Try it to a blues number or a ballad.*

Like all Dancercises, this will stretch, limber, tighten and relax you all over. Most of all, it will give you pleasure in moving and in your own bounteous body.

1-4. *From the 'mermaid' position, roll onto a cushion on the floor. Draw up the top knee and extend leg to the side.* **5**. *Turn torso and leg so face is looking at the floor.* **6**. *Lower leg so foot rests on floor and gently stretch away from it.* **7**. *Sweep extended arm towards the front.* **8**. *Fold legs to the starting position.* **9**. *Sit facing straightened legs, swing legs around and repeat whole exercise on other side.*

Aquacise. *Water is a wonderful place to work out. It supports your entire bulk and leaves you free to move every which way. I heartily recommend swimming, or just being in a pool, as often as possible through your pregnancy.* **1**. *Face away from the poolside holding on behind you with arms spread like the Rolls Royce bonnet girl – an exercise in itself for the shoulders and pectorals. You will bring yourself more or less vertical in the water. Bring one knee up to the surface.* **2**. *Stretch out the leg (not as easy as you think against the pressure of the water).* **3**. *Pull the leg down through the water to the starting point. Repeat with the other leg.* **4**. *On the third go, when the leg is stretched forward, push away from your support with your hands, bring your legs together and hold that beautiful poised angel pose – top of the back arched, head and arms thrown back, body and legs thrust and tapered down towards the depths. Push away. Continue across the pool swimming.*

Swimming itself, along with dance, is the most thorough exercise you can get. Vary your strokes so you use all the muscle groups. This is a side stroke. It is more relaxing than the crawl and enables you to flex and then stretch the legs, arms and back: this and variations on it are excellent for toning stomach muscles.

Post-natal exercises

After the birth. *Well, you have delivered, you are overwhelmed with the terrifying responsibility of a 24-hours-a-day, seven-days-a-week, irreversible – and joyous – charge. You are also despairing over whether that mound you are trying to zip into your trousers will ever disappear. Take courage, new mother, it will. Some will dissolve automatically as the hormones reorder.*

The rest is up to you. Our rule of thumb about when exercise can be resumed or started is six weeks; that is, after your post-natal examination gives you a clean bill of health. Ask your doctor if you want to start before that. Dancers do. Once again, the first movement in your exercise programme is to walk over to your radio or stereo and get the music going. That will get you going too.

Therapy by Terpsichore. *With all the marvellous combinations of movements the body is capable of, there is no reason for limiting your exercise to the monotonous 1-2-3-4 sort. Dancercising will not only provide you with an endless and entertaining variety of movements. It will also inspire you to persist – far more than will the dreary goal of reducing. Nevertheless, you have a lot of shaping*

up to do; postpone it and you will find the sludge increasingly unshiftable.

Try this combination for a warm up – and then create more of your own to beaty disco or rock music. **1.** *Right hand on hip, touch left foot behind as you stretch left arm up.* **2.** *Bend knees, tighten stomach muscles and drop; place left hand on (or, at first, near) the floor.* **3.** *Gripping stomach muscles, come up,*

lifting the left knee. **4.** *Point left foot to the left. Chant: 'stretch, drop, lift, point.' Repeat to the left by stepping on the left foot as you stretch with the right arm. Reverse the instructions by substituting left for right and vice versa. When you come up (fig. 3), be sure you* roll up, *using your stomach, instead of straightening up like a crane, which puts a strain on your back.*

The floor show. *This sequence actually takes only about six feet square. Do it oozily to a ballad or (later) more rapidly to a quickstep. But keep it rhythmical.* **1**. *Stretch out voluptuously from toe to fingertips, pulling abdominal muscles long. Allow your belly to fall into its natural cavity* **2**. *Curving the spine, lift the shoulders, reach the right arm towards the left knee, stomach muscles compressed against the spine. Hold for two counts. Release by returning carefully to the floor and elongating the stomach muscles and spine for two counts. Repeat with the other leg and arm. At first, do 1 and 2 about eight times a day. It is an excellent tummy tightener.* **3**. *Roll knees to the right. Try to keep both shoulders on the floor as long as possible.* **4**. *Stretch legs out to the right side (to 9 o'clock).* **5**. *Swing legs down (to 6 o'clock) as you roll onto your side – not on the hip bone but slightly onto the thigh pad. Bring right arm up, left arm down and make a crescent shape. You have to grip the stomach muscles to hold your balance. (Continued below left).*

(Continued from above right). **6**. *Roll – do not plop – towards the right shoulder onto your stomach. Stretch legs and torso away from your hips.* **7**. *Bend your knees, push on your hands, moving hips towards the right until you are sitting on your left hip* (**8**). **9**. *Continue around to the right until you face forward. N.B. Figures 3-9 take you through a complete circle.* **10**. *Tightening the stomach, reach forward over your legs.* **11**. *Roll back on the floor, bone by bone, controlling your descent with your stomach muscles, until you are:* **12** *stretched out in the starting position. Repeat the whole sequence to the left, substituting left for right in the instructions and vice versa.*

Royal births

The births of the Princess of Wales' two children have illustrated many of the changing attitudes towards this most important of family events. To begin with, childbirth is no longer thought of as rather frightening, painful (Queen Victoria was the first Royal mother to accept aneasthetic) and impersonal. Doctors and maternity hospitals today care for the well-being not just of the mother and child, but of the father and other members of the family as well.

The active role of the father is one of the more important changes of recent years. The father is now often present at the birth – something that would have been unthinkable a generation ago. Prince Charles and Captain Mark Phillips are two of the young Royal fathers who have followed this trend. Prince Charles' birth was more traditional; Prince Philip was playing squash with an equerry at the time. In one respect, however, he did break with tradition. He was the first heir to the throne to be born without the Home Secretary being present – a practice that has now been abandoned, presumably for ever.

The Princess has also demonstrated another modern trend – that of having the baby in hospital rather than at home. Whereas home confinement was once standard practice, except in the case of complications, doctors now prefer all babies to be born in hospital, where the best equipment and qualified care are to hand. Hospital confinement is fairly new in the Royal Family. When the Queen was born by caesarean section on 21st April 1926, the operation was carried out in the home of her parents in Bruton Street in London, not in hospital. Royal babies these days are more likely to be born in the special maternity Lindo wing of St Mary's, Paddington, where both Princess Diana and Princess Anne chose to have their babies, under the watchful eye of obstetrician George Pinker. Prince William's birth was, in fact, the first occasion on which the heir to the throne has been born in a public place. Prince Charles was born at Buckingham Palace, and most other Royal babies since the turn of the century have been born in London. However, Princess Margaret was born at Glamis Castle on 21st August, 1930. When they went to register her at the local post office, they saw that she would be number thirteen; so they waited. Even royalty is superstitious. Other Royal babies have broken with tradition more or less by accident. Prince Andrew was the first child to be born to a reigning monarch since 1857; and Peter Phillips was the first Royal baby to be born a commoner for five hundred years.

Another change in recent times has been that it matters far less whether the baby is a boy or a girl. The Prince and Princess of Wales were clearly delighted with their new son, but they would undoubtedly have been just as enthralled with a daughter. At one time, the woman's main duty was to produce a son and heir. It is reported that, at the birth of Queen Victoria's first child, the Princess Royal, Dr Lacock, the obstetrician said "Oh, your Majesty, it's only a Princess", and Queen Victoria replied "Never mind, next time it will be a Prince".

Some traditions remain. When Prince Henry Charles Albert David was born on the 16th September 1984, an official bulletin was pinned up on the railings at Buckingham Palace, just as it had been for generations before him. The parents rejoiced, and the nation could join in with them.

Baby Fashion

*A cheerful young Prince William, at the age of eighteen months,
sets a Royal fashion trend in his ABC snow-suit as he shows his
paces to the cameras at Christmas 1983.*

Contrasts in children's fashions over the last hundred years. Facing page: Prince Albert Victor of Wales, oldest son of Edward V11, demonstrates the Victorian habit of dressing small boys in clothes that would today be thought entirely effeminate. Below: Princess Anne's daughter, Zara, wears clothes that typify the modern approach to children's fashion. She and her brother Peter, seen here at Windsor in May 1984, could, if it weren't for the age difference, almost swap outfits.

F ashion influences children's clothes as much as it does the clothes that adults wear. And like women's fashions, they fall into two categories; the traditional classics that go on from generation to generation, and today's more informal clothes – 'street fashions' – which include such things as snow suits, track and sweatwear, and dungarees, such as Osh Kosh (a name that has become almost synonymous with children's clothes). Hardly surprisingly, tastes in children's wear seem to reflect the prevailing fashions for their mothers. In this respect, today's young Royal mothers are not so very different from other young mothers: they dress fashionably themselves, and so do their children. Princess Anne's children, Peter and Zara Phillips, are examples: denim cords and jeans, check shirts and colourful sweaters, are typical of the clothes that they can be seen wearing every day. Obviously, there are special occasions when they have to dress in their 'Sunday Best' (see page 60), but in the main they wear casual clothes that are both hard wearing and comfortable. Comfort is very much a modern day consideration for children's clothes. Children detest feeling uncomfortable, or embarrassed by their clothes. No modern child would be seen dead wearing the sort of outfit that Prince Albert Victor of Wales, son of Queen Victoria, was dressed in as a small boy in 1868. It can't have been ideal for playing in either.

A look at today's young members of the Royal family – Prince William, son of the Prince and Princess of Wales; Peter and Zara Phillips; the Earl of Ulster, Lady Davina and Lady Rose, children of the Duke and Duchess of Windsor; and Lord Frederick and Lady Gabriella, son and daughter of Prince and Princess Michael of Kent – reveals a charming cross section of modern children's wear. Individual differences of taste can be seen, but taken together they demonstrate how lively children's fashion has become over the past decade. So also has adult fashion, and this must have been one of the main reasons for the change. Denim has been increasingly popular for both parents and children, and the fabric that was once confined to the workplace is seen more or less everywhere. Alongside this has been the introduction of sportswear worn not only on the sports field, but for every day. Both these trends have helped to create a new relaxed style of dressing, which has followed through strongly into children's clothes.

There is, of course, a need today for more practical clothes than those worn by toddlers of previous generations. Few modern mothers have the time to starch, iron and care for fussy children's clothes. And today's child needs, and demands, to be able to play and move around free from restricting clothing. This means that there is greater use of hard wearing fabrics that are easy to care for. Natural fibres such as wool and cotton still remain favourites, but mixtures of man-made fibres with natural ones provide easy care fabrics that are less expensive, as with the new fashion for sweatshirting fabric which is now used in a whole range of different children's and adult's clothes. Most of the young Royal mothers patronise Viyella, a lightweight 55% wool/45% cotton mix fabric, the first of its kind to be manufactured, which has been traditionally associated with children's wear in the

Prince William at his first official photo' session at Kensington Palace in 1981 wears a smocked romper suit in one of the most traditional styles of babywear.

Royal Family over several generations (it carries the Royal Warrant). However, if the major consideration for everyday children's clothes is that they should be practical, then it is certainly one that is reflected in the clothes worn by young Royal children today.

In the 1980s, Royal children's clothes are much more likely to have come from high street shops and department stores than might have been the case a generation or so ago. The Princess of Wales, for example, is known to shop at a wide variety of places, from Harrods and Marks and Spencer to more specialized central London children's boutiques like Bimbo and Galligans. She is not alone in choosing a cross section of shops in which to buy children's clothes. Princess Anne too has a down-to-earth approach to her children's wardrobes. In other words, Royal children's styles, unlike those of their mothers, are relatively easy for any mother to emulate; and the outfits that are too expensive for most mothers to buy are really quite cheap and simple to make. (See Chapter 4).

Prince William made his first public appearance in one of the more 'classic' of baby outfits – a smocked romper suit very similar to the one his father wore as a baby – and classic clothes have always played a major part in the upbringing of British children, not just Royal ones. Photographs of Princess Elizabeth (the Queen) and her sister Princess Margaret as children often show them wearing double-breasted wool coats with velvet collars: the same style reappeared with both Prince Charles and Princess Anne and, today, it can be seen once again on Peter Phillips and Lord Frederick Windsor. Once the preserve of expensive London stores, such coats can now be bought at reasonable prices from many high street shops (see page 62). Tartan kilts, too, have long been associated with the Royal Family. In fact, Queen Alexandra, mother of Edward V11, thought they were wonderful, as both her sons and her daughters could wear them, which saved on the budget (see page 68). Sailor suits are also very much part of the Royal tradition, virtually unaffected by the vagaries of fashion (see page 70). Other perennials have been fairisle sweaters and cardigans for both boys and girls (see page 58). A fairisle sweater and tartan kilt would be a familiar and appropriate outfit for a holiday at Balmoral.

Babywear

During their first year of life, modern babies have a wide choice of clothes, ranging from the traditional favourites of days gone by to the colourful stretch-fabric playsuits of today. Baby fashions have changed as much as those for adults, if not more, and one of the major changes has been that baby boys are dressed as boys from the start rather than as baby girls. Only a generation or so ago, all babies were dressed alike, regardless of sex, firstly in long dresses and frilled caps and later in skirts, petticoats and frilly dresses. It was not until he was four or five years old that a boy made the sharp transition to masculine attire. The practice of putting toddlers and infants into trousers was unknown before Edwardian times. Today, the pendulum has swung the other way and little girls are often to be seen in clothes that might otherwise have been worn by their brothers. Specialised babywear is really only worn for the first three or four months, if at all. Every

The Princess of Wales broke new ground by taking Prince William on a Royal tour when he was less than a year old. Here, in Australia, he wears the sort of outfit that any baby of his age could crawl and play in in comfort.

mother can make her own choice, as indeed the Princess of Wales has done. Prince William's first public appearance in a traditional smocked romper suit (usually worn by babies up to the age of six to nine months) was followed at the age of nine months, by an appearance in traditional 'crawlers', a two-piece suit with blouse and pants which are secured in the middle by buttons. They are aptly named; babies can crawl in them with comfort and ease. Many of these classic babywear styles in romper suits, dresses and knitwear have been passed down from generation to generation (sometimes even the clothes themselves), and they are unlikely to be superseded in the generations to come.

The first time that most mothers-to-be have to consider baby clothes is when they are preparing the layette. When Prince Charles was born, at a time when much more formal babywear was the fashion, he was given a layette by the Linen and Woollen Drapers Institute consisting of fifty-five garments produced by twenty-five retired dressmakers. This, of course, is rather large by today's standards. Young mothers today are quite likely to depend to a large extent on items of clothing and equipment borrowed from friends or handed down from brothers and sisters, or made by affectionate aunts and mothers-in-law. All the same, every baby needs certain things from the moment he or she

Previous generations of Royal baby girls. Top: Princess Victoria of Wales, granddaughter of Queen Victoria, swathed in the smart baby fashion of the time. Above: a more relaxed but still elaborate outfit for a delightful little Princess Elizabeth of York, later Queen Elizabeth 11.

arrives back home, and it is always useful to have a checklist of the necessities. The following are the contents of a typical layette from, for example, Mothercare: two Cotton wrap-over vests; two Baby's stretch bodysuits with easy-fit envelope necks; two first size all in one baby-stretch suits; two Winceyette baby gowns; two matinee jackets; two hats; two pairs of bootees; two pairs of outdoor mittens; two pairs of scratch mittens; one baby's first blanket; two waterproof backed Terry bibs; one toiletries gift box containing baby powder, baby lotion, baby shampoo and baby soap; one pack of twelve de-luxe absorbent Terry nappies; one pack of twenty-two supersoft fabric nappy liners; one pack of twenty-four all-in-one disposable nappies and pants; one pack of three Ever-dri nappies; one card of six nappy pins; two pairs of long-life luxury waterproof pants; and one packet of nappy sani-tising powder.

The first few weeks are the time when presents are lavished on the baby. Princess Michael of Kent's son, Lord Frederick Windsor, was given a beautiful Christian Dior romper suit by Begum Aga Khan; and many of the clothes Prince Charles wore as a baby were made by his great grandmother, Queen Mary. No doubt Princess Diana received plenty of presents from other members of the Royal Family, as well as a deluge of gifts from the general public – including a book of nursery rhymes entirely made of lace, the product of ten thousand working hours by the lace-makers of Beer in Devon. Apart from knitwear, however, today's baby is mostly given shop bought goods, and it is worth trying to make sure that not all the things that are bought (or made) are for a new-born size baby. Most babies grow out of this size very quickly, and some never fit it at all. Try making and buying for three to six month old sizes. Tiny low-weight or premature babies need special sizes, and many specialised shops and chain stores, including Mothercare, stock clothes in 60 cm (24 inch) sizes; and some mothers have even been known to dress their babies in doll's clothes.

Shop bought clothes, however well made, practical and comfortable they may be, are almost always mass-produced: the art of making beautiful baby clothes is rarely found today, and when it is found it can make the price of such items astronomic and beyond the reach of most young families. The White House in London, who specialise in selling beautiful hand-made babywear say that a romper suit could cost from £70 upwards, depending on the fabric – yet they still remain firm favourites with their customers. The answer for many mothers is to make their own (see page 107 for a dressmaking pattern and instructions for a traditional style romper suit). These traditional clothes are often surprisingly cheap and easy to make.

Despite the trend towards 'unisex' dressing for very young children, dresses remain very much an alternative to such things as romper suits for baby girls; it is worth bearing in mind that a colourful, striped, vest can serve as a dress for a baby girl and then double up as a summer t-shirt for either a boy or a girl. Princess Anne, who is obviously in favour of very practical children's clothes, often put her daughter Zara in dresses from an early age. Princess Elizabeth of York (later the Queen), among other little Royal girls of previous genera-tions, was always seen in dresses, usually rather more flamboyant than those seen today. She didn't start wearing more practical less formal clothes until she was much older. Going back to Victorian times, tastes were even more extreme. Queen Victoria's grand-daughter, Princess Victoria of Wales (seen opposite as a baby in the arms of her nurse Mrs Quinlan), would often have been put into dresses very like her mother's. In the past, fashions in babywear tended to reflect the most inappropriate aspects of adult fashion. Unfortunately for them, and probably for their mothers as well, babies and young children were often forced into the cumbersome and restricting styles that their parents wore. They must have been uncomfortable as well as impractical. Modern babies are luckier. Where children's styles have borrowed from adult fashion, they have drawn on its most practical and comfortable aspect, and take full account of the infant's need to grow and move around freely.

There is no doubt, however, that the major fashion change in recent years has been the introduction of all-in-one 'sleepsuits', such as the Babygro, for boys and girls alike. They have become an essential part of a baby's wardrobe, and even part of the layette. An example of this type of outfit is the pair of blue velour baby dungarees, with a cream t-shirt style sweater underneath, which was worn by Princess Michael of Kent's son, Frederick. The outfit is typical of the ones you can see on many young babies of both sexes. They are usually made in velour or stretch cotton and vary in price according to fabric and design. They are for night as well as day and have largely replaced the traditional Winceyette nightgown, although these are still favoured by some Royal mothers. With these all-in-one suits, there is little need for bootees. In fact, fashion today favours baby socks rather than the traditional bootees. Never rush a baby into proper shoes; the experts say that they are not needed until the baby is walking.

These changes in style are not the only dramatic developments in babywear. Colour has also become enormously more important. White is, and always has been, a firm favourite as have the traditional pastel baby pinks and blues and lemon (particularly popular in the late '20s when women wore such shades as apricot, peach, pale mint green and cream). But today's colours in babywear are far less rigid and such sharper and bolder colours as navy, red and burgundy – echoing modern fashion trends – are common. The Princess of Wales dressed her son in traditional pastel shades during his early months, but she showed a taste for darker shades and brighter colours as he grew older. One favourite was the ABC ski-suit which Prince William wore during the winter of 1983/1984 (see page 41). This was made in dark blue rather than traditional baby blue and lined with bright red – a combination very much in keeping with the trend towards more colourful children's clothes generally. With these stronger colours, it is often a good idea is to combine them with contrasting colours to highlight them. For example, if you are dressing a baby in dark brown then choose a cream t-shirt or sweater to go with it, much as you would if you were picking accessories for one of your own outfits. A popular new colour is very light grey, which mixes attractively with lemon, pink or baby blue, and has the advantage of suiting both boys and girls (useful when buying clothes for an as yet unborn baby). Remember that children, even at a very early age, have their own distinctive colouring, both in their hair and in their complexions. It is important to dress them in colours that set off their own colouring and enhance their natural health so that they look fresh and well.

Modern generations of Royal baby boys. Top: Prince Charles at the age of one, displaying his recently acquired teeth, is dressed in a smart but simple and unfussy outfit. Above: Lord Frederick Windsor, with his mother, Princess Michael of Kent, shows how today's Royal Family have adopted the trend to colourful and practical babywear.

Baby knitwear

Snapshots from the Royal Family album, like those of any other family, emphasise how little has changed in knitwear fashions. Above left: Prince William looks warm and comfortable in his woollen hat and leggings on his return from New Zealand after the Royal Tour in 1983. Above right: A delightful picture of Princess Alexandra as a baby shows her wearing a typical baby cardigan, one of the most ageless of designs. Modern versions might use stronger colours and perhaps patterns, rather than pale pastels or white, but the basic design would be recognisable to any mother in any era.

As long as there are grandmothers and aunts who are handy with a knitting needle, knitwear will remain standard in the baby's wardrobe. The styles don't change much from generation to generation. Matinee jackets, shawls, hats and legging suits – like the one worn by Prince William (above) – have probably been worn by babies since knitting was first invented. And while such clothes can easily be bought, they remain a favourite present from relatives to the new born baby, and hand-knitting is still very much the rule.

Hats and bonnets are other traditional knitted items of babywear, and little thumbless mittens can be useful, not only to keep the baby's hands warm, but to stop them scratching. Hats and bonnets are essential for any outdoor trip in the fresh air on a cold or chilly day. More heat escapes from the baby's head than from any other part of the body. The Queen Mother's daughters wore bonnets throughout their early childhood. The Queen, then Princess Elizabeth of York, had at least a hundred and her nurse used to change them at least twice a day. The Queen, in turn, often dressed her own daughters in them, although Princess Anne has not followed suit with her daughter Zara. Prince William has worn a hat, but one that is much more typical of today's fashion in baby headgear. The modern pull-on, close-fitting style, with ear-flaps that fasten under the chin and probably a pom-pom, is less fussy than the traditional bonnet as well as being warmer and more practical because it is easily washed.

Shawls, too, are traditionally part of the baby's layette. Beautifully knitted or crocheted, they are sometimes almost works of art. Here again, shawls have become a little outmoded, and baby 'sleeping nests' or sleeping bags are often used instead. But for a new-born baby, there is still no substitute for the beautifully wrought, soft, comforting, warm, woollen shawl.

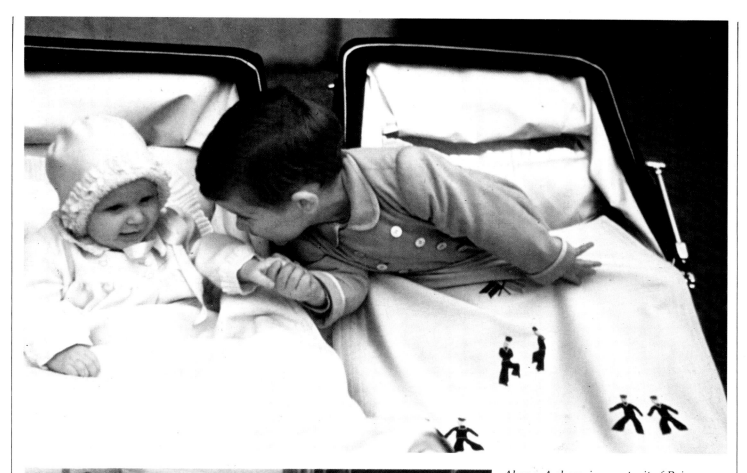

Above: A charming portrait of Prince Charles and his little sister, Princess Anne, wearing the traditional bonnet as protection against the cold. Left: the Queen as a child had over a hundred bonnets, changed twice a day. Here, she is seen about to set out for a drive in the park.

Prince William arrives for the annual Royal holiday at Balmoral Castle in August 1984 wearing a pair of colourful blue shorts and smock-trimmed white shirt – unruffled by his long flight.

Everyday casuals

Today's toddler or young child is likely to be dressed in casual clothes most, if not all, of the time. Again, fashions in young children's wear tend to reflect the current fashions for their parents and as a result the emphasis is now on casual, simple and highly practical outfits. However, the vagaries of adult fashion tend to show up less in terms of style – styles in children's wear are much less changeable than those for women – and more in terms of fabric and colour, and in attitudes towards children's clothes generally. Corduroy and denim have been popular for children for many years, but as new fabrics such as sweatshirting become fashionable, so they become widely adopted for the very young. This has been particularly noticeable since the move into sports-influenced clothes, such as jogging suits. The main attraction of this type of fabric as opposed to the more traditional ones is, of course, that it is washable and easy to care for – a major consideration for any busy mother. Colours, too, can demonstrate that fashion is fickle, even in children's wear. One year, the high street shops will be flooded with bright, colourful, patterned clothes whereas the year before they might have been dominated by softer and quieter shades of brown and navy blue.

Perhaps the most important change of all, however, has been the change in our whole attitude to the way we dress our children. The modern Royal child, like all other children, is treated as a child, and dressed as one. It is highly unlikely, for example, that the Princess of Wales has plans to dress Prince William in the sort of tailored suit that his father wore as a child. He is much more likely to appear in a t-shirt and jeans. Even this was less formal than the three-piece suit that King George V was obliged to wear as a child. The only concession to his tender years appears to have been that he was allowed to wear short trousers. The difference today is not so much that children's fashion doesn't continue to echo adult fashion but that it has seized on a more appropriate aspect of adult fashion to follow. A portrait of Queen Victoria at the age of four shows her dressed more like a middle-aged woman than a child – a perfect example of the Victorian habit of treating small children as miniature adults rather than as children in their own right.

Dungarees, jeans, t-shirts and shorts have become very much the uniform of today's child; not just for boys but for girls as well. There has, in fact, been a genuine revolution in fashion for little girls, so that they are now wearing all the clothes that were once reserved for small boys. And very pretty they can look. A small girl in a soft, pretty, pastel-coloured pair of dungarees with a flowered t-shirt underneath, or in denims with a fun t-shirt, can look enormously appealing. Don't worry if they are too long – they can look just as good rolled up. As with women's clothes, the art of dressing children well lies in keeping things simple, and what could be simpler, more practical or more durable than a pair of dungarees? (See page 116 for a pattern and exclusive design). There are, of course, many variations on this theme. Prince William made a memorable appearance on his second birthday – incidentally demonstrating to the assembled British press that he was every bit as curious and inquisitive as any other two year old – wearing an outfit with a bib top and shorter-cut trousers, the summer

Prince William at the age of two, and a painting of his great-great-great-great grandmother at the age of four. William, happily playing on the occasion of his second birthday photographic session, looks a great deal more comfortable than the little Victoria.

version of the dungarees, and a style that could be found in many of the leading chain stores.

Trousers for women started to become fashionable during the second world war, so it is no surprise to find them now an essential part of a small girl's wardrobe. The first of the Royal children to follow the trend was Princess Anne. She and Prince Charles were often dressed alike throughout their childhood. Both were seen, for example, in knitted double-breasted cardigans and corduroy pants. It is said that Prince Philip himself insisted that his daughter should break with the tradition of wearing neat kilts and pretty dresses all the time and should instead wear more relaxed clothes like trousers and jerseys. Things were not the same for the Queen or Princess Margaret – neither was ever seen in overalls or dungarees. Now that the barriers have broken down, most mothers prefer to dress their children alike,

Royal brothers and sisters, dressed casually and alike. Above: Prince Charles and Princess Anne, in 1952 at Balmoral, wear perfect examples of the 'unisex' fashions of the time. Anne's cord trousers clearly echo the growing popularity of trousers for women after the Second World War. Right: Peter and Zara Phillips in the modern equivalent at Windsor in May 1983 – dungarees for both boys and girls.

Above left: rather more grown up, but still in look-alike fashion, Prince Charles and Princess Anne disembark for a picnic in South Uist, in the Outer Hebrides, in 1956. Lady Diana Spencer, with her younger brother Charles (above right), despite her known preference for more feminine clothes, was not above dressing in a pair of shorts to match her brother's.

regardless of sex. Princess Anne has no doubt inherited some of her father's preferences. Little Zara often wears dungarees, shirts and jeans that are virtually identical to those worn by her older brother Peter. And although Princess Diana was known to have a preference for pretty dresses, she was often seen wearing t-shirts and shorts like her younger brother Charles. No doubt she will continue the trend as her own family grows up.

Clothes for small children need not be expensive. Many high street stores stock fashionable clothes at reasonable prices, and the competent seamstress can easily make them herself. (See Chapter 4). There is also the great advantage that the sort of casual clothes that are in fashion today can be worn throughout the year. There is nothing seasonal about dungarees, jeans, shirts, sweatshirts or even t-shirts. Nevertheless, children grow at a remarkable rate. If you buy something rather special, there is a very good chance that it will get very little wear before it is thrown away because it has been outgrown. It is always worth bearing in mind the various ways of extending the life of these clothes. One useful technique is to buy clothes that are slightly too large, and turn up the hemline, or add an extra tuck,

A practical rather than fussy approach for little Zara Phillips, seen here with her mother at the Windsor Horse Trials in June 1984. This charming blue sundress shows off the best of modern styling for children.

which can then be let out again at a later stage. Since the fashion trend is anyway towards more casual 'fun' clothes, don't be worried about dressing your child in clothes that are a bit too big for them – much better than dressing them in something too tight. Children can look very appealing, especially around the age of three when most of the baby fat has gone and they have slimmed down a bit, in outfits that are slightly on the large size for them. (Be careful, however, of doing this with very young babies, especially when they are beginning to crawl, since over-large clothes can be cumbersome.) Try adding a fun belt or braces to a pair of jeans-style trousers, which can work well for either a boy or a girl; and for girls, try a large size sweatshirt worn as a dress. But be careful of extras that might prove dangerous to small children. Ties and scarves may look very pretty, but in play they could be dangerous or even lethal. Tights and colourful socks are, of course. quite safe, and children love to wear them. Long brightly coloured or patterned socks, worn with lace-ups or trainers, look good on both boys and girls, and even on toddlers. And when a pair of short trousers does finally become too short, then provided that it isn't too tight as well, you can tuck them into long coloured socks or leg warmers to make a warm winter outfit.

Layered clothes can also look extremely good on children. For example, try a pair of dungarees, or a pinafore dress for a girl, with a checked shirt and a t-shirt underneath; or a pair of trousers with a long-sleeved t-shirt and a slipover or top. This is also one of the best ways of making certain clothes wearable all the year round. In winter, a pinafore dress in a darker fabric or in a pattern such as a tartan can be invaluable. It can be worn with a t-shirt, sweater or shirt underneath and even, for extra warmth, with a waistcoat on top.

For those little girls who want to wear dresses rather than jeans, there are plenty of alternatives to the traditional little 'frock'. Take, for example, the pretty blue-striped sundress that Zara Phillips wore at Windsor in June 1984. This is a dress that shows off the best of modern styling for children. The design is simple as well as practical because it can be worn either on its own or doubled up with a pinafore. Note the sensible t-bar shoes by Start-rite, holders of the Royal Warrant, who are also known to supply Prince William's shoes. The Princess of Wales is thought to have to buy several pairs at a time, not just because of normal wear and tear, but because, word has it, the Prince likes to dispose of them by flushing them down the lavatory.

Finally, there is still what is perhaps the most traditional way of dressing children of them all – in hand-me-downs. Certainly, with children's growth patterns so erratic and unpredictable, it makes a great deal of sense to buy things that can be used for other children when, often all too soon, they are outgrown by their owner. With clothes that are hardly worn, but have lost their crispness and colour, you can always dye them. Use one of the machine washable dyes (providing the fabric is washable in the first place) and follow the instructions carefully. And if a child's dress fits your small daughter perfectly but is a little too short, you can add a row of broderie anglaise around the hem. This works on velvet and tartans as well as cotton. The Royal Family are no strangers to such practices. The Queen often had items of clothing let down, or new collars and cuffs sewn onto old clothes. The habit is not just a thrifty one; it is pure common sense.

The Royal Trendsetters

Royal children, like their parents, have always set new fashion trends. This is not because they have been particularly creative, or even innovative, in the things they wear. The Royal Family tend to set the seal of approval on new fashions, rather than creating them. It is simply a consequence of who they are. The ones most constantly in the public eye are, of course, the most influential: Prince William has already had an effect on the baby fashion scene – as did his father before him – and with the benefit of his mother's flair for clothes, he will undoubtedly soon be leading trends in older children's wear. It won't be long before the new Royal baby will also be wearing clothes with a fashion element. Diana's children may yet have as big an impact in their own areas of fashion as she did in hers.

Prince William began to demonstrate his own influence at an early stage. One of his most imitated garments was the dark blue snow-suit, with an ABC motif, which he wore during the winter of 1983/1984. (See page 41.) Before long, the streets were full of push-chairs containing small children in snow-suits of a very similar style. Another of his successful outfits, although perhaps less well known, was a 'fun' picture motif anorak, which has also had its imitators.

Obviously, such clothes as these reflect Princess Diana's own liking for bold, striking picture sweaters, and this type of picture pattern or appliqué motif can look very appealing and effective on children's clothes. Unfortunately, items like these do tend to belong to the rather more individual and exclusive styles that would be found in a top department store such as Harrods or in specialised children's boutiques. They can be expensive. However, it is possible to achieve a similar effect rather more cheaply. You can now buy quite a wide range of motifs from most haberdashers which can easily be sewn onto a pair of dungarees or an anorak, or onto a plain sweater or sweatshirt. This can be a good way of turning a simple top into something more individual and colourful. Do make sure that the motif fabric is washable (assuming that the garment is too), otherwise you will have to take it off each time the clothes are washed. And, of course, where knitwear is concerned, you can always do it yourself. Attractive patterns are available, and one of them is given on page 112 in Chapter 4. In other words, it need not be an expensive business keeping up with Royal children's fashion.

Prince Charles, in his day, also started early as a trend-setter. At the age of four, he was named one of the 'World's Top Ten Best Dressed Men' by *The Tailor and Cutter* magazine, who praised his taste in baby bows, farm stalkers and double-breasted woollies. The magazine also made the comment that "His velvet-collared top coat also follows a popular current trend." This type of coat has been a favourite for Royal children for many years, and indeed it still is. (See page 62). Charles made the list again when he was six years old, but since then, comments on his clothes have usually been rather less kind. The Queen too showed signs of being a fashion leader when she was only three. The discovery that her nursery clothes and trimmings were yellow caused great excitement, particularly in America. *Time* magazine appeared with a front cover that bore a portrait of Princess Elizabeth and a caption that proclaimed " 'P'INCESS LILYBET' *She has*

The Princess's love of bright, colourful casual clothes shows up in her choice for William of this appliquéd anorak. Will he be a leader of fashion as his mother has become?

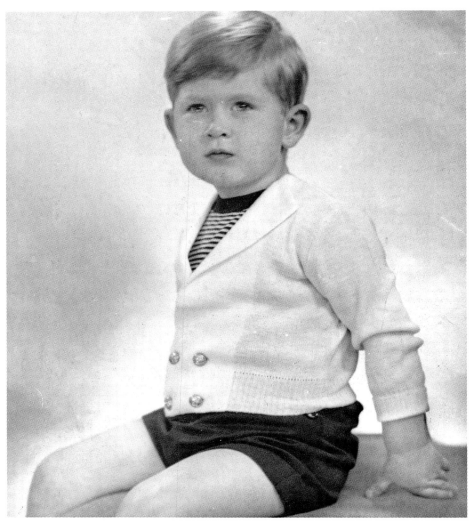

Above: Pink for young Peter Phillips, a departure from tradition in clothes for small boys. This quilted gilet, white sweater and pants makes an ideal and attractive outfit for an outdoor occasion like Badminton in 1983, and a bold choice for his mother, Princess Anne. Right: one of the 'World's Ten Best Dressed Men', as chosen by the Tailor and Cutter Magazine *in 1952, at the age of four. The magazine praised his taste in baby bows, farm stalkers and double breasted woollies. Facing page: the Queen herself was another Royal trendsetter, achieving the ultimate accolade of a front cover feature of* Time *magazine at the age of three. The discovery that her nursery clothes and fittings were all in yellow caused great excitement on both sides of the Atlantic.*

set the babe fashion for yellow.". And in Selfridges department store in London's Oxford Street, there was a booming trade in the coveted little yellow outfits that customers had to order specially for their children. Even earlier, in the 19th century, it was the young Edward V11 who set the trend for one of the most enduring of Royal fashion traditions in children's wear – the sailor suit. When he first wore it in public, the Commander-in-Chief of the navy sent a signal saying "The Navy is delighted. God bless our little admiral." Others were presumably delighted as well, for the sailor suit has endured as a popular, and a Royal, favourite to this day. (See page 70).

Finally, it would be a great mistake to forget or underestimate the other Royal children, Prince William's cousins. Perhaps because there is less media coverage of them, it often goes unnoticed that they wear quite *avant garde* clothes. Take, for example, Peter Phillips, Princess Anne's son. Dressed in a fairisle sweater and cords on one day, he appears on another in white pants, white sweater and a pale pink quilted gilet. It is hard to imagine his grandfather or great-grandfather wearing such informal clothes or such unorthodox colours. But they are typical of the modern trends in children's wear; the trends that have produced today's wide variety of colourful, comfortable and practical clothes for all, including Royal, children.

FIFTEEN CENTS

April 29, 1929

TIME

The Weekly Newsmagazine

Volume XIII

"P'INCESS LILYBET"
She has set the babe fashion for yellow.
(See FOREIGN NEWS)

Number 17

Knitwear

Knitwear dominates the fashion scene today. In women's fashion as much as in children's there has been a revolution in knitted clothes. In the past few years, modern design has had a strong effect on knitwear and made it one of the most exciting areas of current fashion. The range of patterns and styles that can be hand-made or bought is constantly expanding.

Children have always been greater wearers of knitwear than adults. In the past they have often been dressed from head to toe in knitted outfits. Woollen sweaters would be matched with knitted trousers or skirts, with knitted hats, gloves and socks to complete the ensemble. Prince Charles as a child wore outfits of this sort – for example a patterned sweater with matching plain pants (far right). They were typical of the knitted looks of the 1950s, and may well have been among the first of their kind to be knitted on a machine. The advanced technology of modern knitting machines is mainly responsible for the enormous range of high quality knitwear now available in the shops, representing all the classic designs in a wide variety of colours.

There is a strong trend today towards rougher and chunkier looks in knitwear, a return to the hand-knitted look as opposed to the plainer sweaters of a few years ago. But the popular British classics – the fairisles, guernseys and arans – still remain at the forefront of children's fashion. (See page 110 for a pattern and knitting instructions for a classic fairisle sweater). Just how popular these are, and have been, can be judged from a look at young members of the Royal Family, both past and present. Prince Edward on his second birthday (near right) and again when a bit older (below right) wears fairisle sweaters of a type that would be familiar to many modern children. Young Peter Phillips (facing page) one of the leaders of knitwear fashion among today's Royal children, is often seen in different jumpers, from ski-style cardigans to chunky, cable knitted slipovers. If you don't much like the plainer styles, a good way of livening them

Prince Edward in classic fairisle, 1966.

A picture sweater for Prince Charles.

Prince Edward, again in timeless fairisle, in Norway in August 1969.

up is to change the buttons, replacing them with brighter colours or even fun animal-shaped ones. Knitted accessories can also be fun. Scarves, pull-on hats and gloves (best attached to a long string threaded through the arms so that they don't get lost) look bright and colourful.

Just as interesting, perhaps even more so, has been the fashion for picture sweaters or motif knits (especially hand knitted), which has been such a prominent part of the knitwear revolution. The Princess of Wales, herself, was one of the leaders of this particular fashion development, with her 'Black Sheep', 'Australian' and other colourful sweaters. One of the safest predictions that can be made about the clothes that Prince William and his new playmate will be wearing is that there will be at least a few items of colourful knitwear. The drawback to these motif sweaters is that they can be rather expensive to buy, and sometimes quite difficult to find. One good alternative, as with picture anoraks and so on (see page 55), is to buy a small motif and appliqué it on to a sweater. This can be particularly useful as a way of covering up a hole caused by wear, or perhaps a burn mark. On the other hand, motif sweaters are not necessarily that difficult to make. Sally Muir and Jo Osborne, of Warm and Wonderful, who designed the Princess's 'Black Sheep' jersey, have designed a 'semi-educational' picture sweater for both boys and girls, and instructions for making it are given on page 112. This is an excellent example of how knitwear has changed its image, and the effects can only be to the good. The more colour and comfort that can be introduced into children's clothes, the better it will be for both them and their parents.

Classic knitwear for young children, demonstrated here by Princess Anne's children, Peter and Zara Phillips. Above left: Zara in an aran on her second birthday at the Windsor Horse Trials. Left and far left: Peter, in a cable knit slipover and heavy patterned wool cardigan. Both represent the trend towards a more hand-knitted and chunkier style of children's knitwear.

Sunday best

Most children have at least one smart outfit which is reserved for special occasions, particularly as they get a bit older. For boys it might be a black blazer, shirt and tie, and short or long trousers. For girls it would probably be a party dress. It is not so common now for families to dress at their smartest to attend church on a Sunday, but the name 'Sunday best' lingers on, and there are plenty of other reasons for wearing it. Christenings, weddings, birthday parties and more formal functions that they might attend with their parents, are all occasions on which children would be likely to need their very smartest clothes.

Royal children obviously have more opprtunities than most to wear Sunday best clothes. A Royal line-up at Windsor Castle on Christmas day several years ago – with Prince Charles and Princess Anne trying to keep the younger ones under control – demonstrates the classic tradition of smart dressing for young children. The same general approach can be seen on many different occasions. The Trooping of the Colour ceremony always brings out some smart young Royals, as do more public family events such as weddings. Prince William wore a very smart pale blue shirt with tiny ruffle front and toning shorts at the Trooping of the Colour ceremony in June 1984. The outfit was quite grown up for the young Prince, but nonetheless very traditional in style. It is interesting to see that the Princess dressed her son in colours that not only matched the ones that she was wearing herself, but also toned in with the outfits worn by the Queen Mother and

A smart turn out for Royal children, on the occasion of the annual Christmas service at St George's Chapel Windsor in 1969 – all dressed in similar style and demonstrating the continuity of Royal style in smart children's clothes. The line up, from left to right, includes James Ogilvy, the Earl of St Andrews, Lady Helen Windsor, Viscount Linley, Prince Andrew, Marina Ogilvy and Prince Edward.

Princess Margaret. This is an idea that any mother could adopt for a suitable occasion, for example a family wedding.

Dressing their children in toning colours is something that the young Royal mothers seem to do quite often. The Duchess of Gloucester's two eldest children, the Earl of Ulster and Lady Davina, were dressed in the same colours when they attended the christening of their younger sister, Lady Rose. Lady Davina wears a pretty soft blue pinafore style dress and a white top with a frilled neck – a simple outfit but a very charming one. Her brother too looks neat and smart in a Peter Pan collared shirt and knee-length trousers. Both outfits have a slightly 'Edwardian' feel to them, without being at all old-fashioned. They are styles of the kind called 'Modern Classics', not likely to date and always suitable for a special occasion.

A rather more traditional outfit, with a definite historic air about it, was the knickerbocker suit worn by Lord Frederick Windsor, Prince and Princess Michael of Kent's son, on his fourth birthday. It has a matching waistcoat and tailored shirt, and is complete with buckled shoes. This might be a little cumbersome, and expensive, for the average four year old, but it would make an excellent page-boy type of outfit for a wedding. The conventional smart outfit for slightly older boys – the blazer, long trousers and shirt and tie – is also often worn by Royal children. Peter Phillips seemed in high spirits wearing just such an outfit when attending church with his parents, Princess Anne and Captain Mark Phillips.

Generally, it is important to remember that most small children are quite excited by smart occasions and enjoy dressing up. They like to feel a bit grown up. It is a good idea to let them look a little more adult than they would the rest of the time. Apart from anything else, it might persuade them to behave in a rather more adult fashion. Certainly, they don't appreciate clothes that err in the opposite direction and look too babyish. Such things can horribly embarrass even quite young children, which will hardly improve the occasion for either you or them.

'Sunday best' outfits for Royal children. Top: Lord Frederick Windsor and parents attending the Christmas day service at Windsor Chapel in 1982, in a very practical hooded coat, with a pair of knickerbockers to add 'period' flavour. Above: Peter Phillips, more formal than usual in a school uniform style of outfit, again for Christmas day at Windsor in 1983. Far left: Prince William's dusky blue tones well with the colours worn by his mother and great-grandmother at the Trooping of the Colour Ceremony in June 1984. Left: the Duchess of Gloucester adopted a similar approach when dressing her two older children, the Earl of Ulster and Lady Davina, in matching pale blue at the christening of their younger sister, Lady Rose.

Royal-style coats

The Royal fashion in children's coats was established as far back as the early '30s, and has hardly changed since. The chosen style is, of course, the velvet-collared coat. With minor variations, this has been seen on almost every young Royal, whether male or female, for the past fifty years. The velvet-collared coat has become a truly British tradition. No doubt Prince William will wear one too when he is old enough. Although the Princess likes to dress her son in modern casual styles, she also appreciates the trusted classics. When the Queen and Princess Margaret were children, they wore several versions of this rather smart double-breasted coat, and their cousins Prince Edward and Princess Alexandra were often dressed in them as well. Such coats were, in fact, considered to be a new fashion in those days. Note the one-bar shoes, often with a button fastening, which were a very popular style at the time. This type of coat has remained very much the same over the years. What changes there have been have been much more variations of detail – velvet collars, plaited collars or wider cut revers – or of fabric – a tweed fabric or dog-tooth check rather than plain wool – than changes to the basic style. The version worn by Prince Charles at the age of three was a very soft peach coloured double-breasted coat trimmed in white, with pearl lock buttons. The colour combination was quite daring for a small boy at the time, and it had a noticeable effect on the fashionable colours for boy's wear for some time afterwards.

Today, coats like these are still widely available and are stocked by many stores, from Harrods at the more expensive end of the range to Marks and Spencer at the less expensive. Good coats, however, are never cheap, and wise mothers always buy them with plenty of room for growth and with good hems on them. Children need to get plenty of wear out of them to justify the investment.

Another style of coat that has become something of a Royal tradition is the girl's cape. A particularly delightful version of this

Princess Elizabeth and Princess Margaret wearing Royal-style overcoats.

was worn by Lady Davina, daughter of the Duke and Duchess of Gloucester (see overleaf). On the same occasion, her brother too looked rather distinguished in his double-breasted city-gent style overcoat, rounded off with a 'cloth' cap. Both these outfits belong to the 'classics' which may change in colour and fabric but hardly at all in style.

A warm velvet-collared coat for young Prince Charles with his mother in 1950.

The young Princess Alexandra and brother Edward.

Prince Charles in the garden of Clarence House in 1951.

Prince Edward and Lady Sarah Armstrong-Jones, 1970.

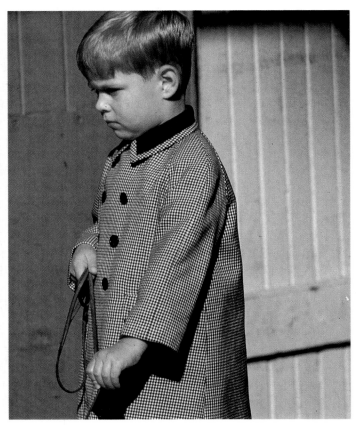

Prince Andrew, in blue and grey check coat, 1964.

Prince Edward and Lady Sarah Armstrong-Jones, 1968

Lady Rose Windsor, a new version of the Royal coat

Lady Davina Windsor, with her brother, in a delightful blue velvet cape, a traditional favourite for little girls.

Party Frocks

Most little girls adore dressing up, particularly in a pretty frock. They don't have to be going to a party or on a special outing; a visit to granny or a favourite aunt will do just as well. Royal little girls are no different, and while there is plenty of time for them to romp around in jeans or a t-shirt, there are always special occasions when they (and no doubt their mothers as well) want something more feminine and appealing. 'Sunday best' frocks these days tend to be less frilly than those of the past, when they were made of nylon or tulle, often in a rather frothy style that would not suit today's young ladies at all. Instead, simple, rather 'period' style, dresses have become fashionable. Drop-waist dresses with tiered skirts; velvet smock dresses with broderie anglaise trims; and traditional smock-style Viyella dresses all make delightful, unfussy and practical outfits for small girls.

The modern way is not to go for anything too dramatic. You will find that detail is restricted to the collar, or a sash belt, or smocking on the bodice. Of course, you can always make a plain dress prettier by buying a ready-made embroidered or lace collar – rather similar, in fact, to the ones that the Princess of Wales favours. They are easily available in most haberdashery stores and departments. Another good way of improvising a special touch to a dress is to make a sash belt out of wide ribbon and then, if suitable, use a matching piece of coloured ribbon as a hair accessory. Most little girls thoroughly enjoy this kind of dressing up. Sometimes, a simple pinafore dress can double up as party wear (see page 61), particularly if it is worn with a soft blouse underneath rather than a sweater, and you could even try a little cotton lace petticoat underneath so that it peeps below the hem.

If you find that shop-bought dresses are rather expensive, then try making one from the pattern, given on page 119, for a traditional-style dress for little girls. Depending on the fabric chosen, this would do either for every day or as a party dress. For summer, cotton and

Zara at the Trooping of the Colour, 1984.   Her mother, Princess Anne, in 1954.

66

broderie anglaise are both excellent fabrics for party dresses, whereas in winter velvet or Viyella are ideal. You will find that many of the other man-made fabrics are also highly suitable.

Royal daughters obviously enjoy dressing up as much as other little girls. Zara, Princess Anne's daughter could be seen at the Trooping of the Colour in 1984 in a traditional-style dress with smock bodice detail, not so very different from the one worn by Marina Ogilvy on her third birthday in 1969, or even the one that Princess Anne often wore as a young girl – although this, with its rather stiff skirt and fitted bodice, is more formal than the modern generation of children would wear. All of them look happy and pretty, as indeed they should. And remember that dressing up your little daughter should be as much fun for you as it is for her.

Party frocks fit for young Princesses. Facing page, top: Zara Phillips in the arms of her mother, wearing a smocked front blue dress. Left: Princess Elizabeth in the frothy style of party dress typical of the time. Below left: a young Princess Alexandra and (below right) her daughter Marina Ogilvy dressed for her fourth birthday party: both demonstrating how little girls love dressing up.

Kilts

A kilted Victorian Prince, the start of a tradition....

...continued a generation on, with less flamboyance.

It is said that kilts, the second most romantic fashion of the 19th century (the first being the sailor suit), also owe their popularity to the Royal Family. After the Jacobite rebellion of 1745, kilts, along with other items of highland dress, were proscribed. After a decent interval, the ban was lifted but for quite some time the kilt was worn by nobility and gentry rather than by highlanders. The fashion really only took off after Prince Albert bought Balmoral Castle in the 1850s, and began to dress Royal children in tartans. Suddenly, tartans were in vogue, not just for kilts but for jackets, waistcoats and hats as well. They have remained popular ever since although, outside the Royal Family and the older

Scottish families, they are more often worn by girls than by boys.

In the Royal Family, kilts tend to be reserved for special occasions – a visit to Balmoral or to the Braemar Games, for example. Both the Queen and Princess Margaret wore them as children, and carried on doing so when they were older. Tartans are reported to be the Queen's favourite item of dress. Prince Charles and Princess Anne certainly wore them at the Braemar Games during their own childhood. The Queen has her own tartan, called Balmoral, which has very delicate colourings of grey, lavender and burgundy. It cannot be bought or worn by anyone else. She is also entitled to wear the Royal Stuart tartan, as are her servants.

Prince Charles has worn this as well as several other tartans, including hunting Lord of the Isles, hunting Stuart and Ancient Stuart. At present, neither Prince William nor Princess Diana have a specific tartan to wear.

Kilts for girls have remained very popular, although they do tend to go in and out of fashion quite rapidly (as does tartan itself). They can be quite expensive to buy, yet they are very easy to make (see page 122 for dress-making instructions). And they certainly need not be confined to girls. Young boys can look very smart in kilts, as Peter Phillips demonstrated at the wedding of his aunt Sarah Phillips in 1982. They make delightful page boy outfits.

Tartans and kilts are perennial Royal favourites. Left: the Queen and Princess Margaret. Top: Prince Charles and Princess Anne at the Braemar Games. Above: Peter Phillips at the wedding of his aunt Sarah Phillips in 1982.

Sailor Suits

One of the most enduring of Royal traditions is dressing young princes, and occasionally princesses, in sailor suits. The tradition dates back to Victorian times. It was evolved for the elder sons of Queen Victoria, who were dressed in an adaptation of the uniforms worn by seamen of the Royal Navy. The earliest sailor suits were usually made of white cloth, with bell-bottomed trousers, pullover tunic and wide-collared kerchief. The outfit was completed by a broad-brimmed straw hat of the type that sailors used to wear.

As the photographs here show, most Royal children seem, at one time or another, to have dressed in sailor suits. Prince Edward (later Edward V11), and his brother Prince Albert were, of course, the founders of the style and gave it its initial popularity. Edward's son (George V) carried on the tradition, although in a rather less elaborate manner. Also seen here is Princess Mary (Queen Mary) with her brothers Prince Albert (George V1) and Prince Edward (Edward V111), showing that it was not only boys who wore sailor suits. Accessories were obviously important; the sailor-style hat tilted to one side takes the place of any other form of cap or bonnet, and heavy lace-up booties were essential footwear.

In recent years, the sailor suit has lost none of its popularity. When Prince Charles at the age of five went to meet his parents in Gibraltar he wore a version of the sailor suit modified to suit the fashions of the day – with full length trousers and a blazer-style 'reefer' jacket over the tunic. And an '80s version, in navy and pale blue rather than white, was seen at the Trooping of the Colour Ceremony in 1981, worn by young Lord Frederick, son of Prince and Princess Michael of Kent. Today, the sailor suit has become rather a formal outfit for boys, although it remains an influence on every day clothes for girls; but it will probably not be long before Prince William too is seen in a sailor suit, the latest upholder of a Royal tradition that is, by now, several generations old. (For full details of how to make a sailor suit for a boy or girl see page 125.)

A gallery of Royal sailor suits, from Victorian times to the present day. The style has proved particularly appropriate to a Royal Family that has always had close connections with the 'senior service' – the navy – and has remained a standard item of children's wear to the present day. Above left; the Duke of York (George V1), at the age of five, at Osborne House. Above; three of George V's children, Princes Albert and Edward, and Princess Mary. The two brothers stand strictly to attention at the salute, in proper naval style. Far left; Prince Charles on a visit to his father in Gibraltar in 1954. Middle left; a portrait by Winterhaller, now in the Royal Gallery at Buckingham Palace, of Queen Victoria's son Prince Edward. Near left; an angelic George V rings the changes by wearing his sailor suit with a straw boater rather than the usual sailor's hat.

The Christening

Christenings in the Royal Family are much like christenings everywhere, in that their primary purpose is the introduction of the child to the Church. The christian names are sometimes longer and more numerous, drawn from family tradition and ancestors through the centuries, and the list of Godparents may be more substantial; but the service is still essentially a religious and traditional one. In the case of the heir to the throne, the religious significance is, perhaps, greater than usual since the British Monarch is – and has been since the time of Henry V111 – the head of the Church of England. The christening of a future King of England is the first spiritual experience of the future defender of the Anglican faith.

The traditional Royal christening robe, worn by Lady Rose Windsor, daughter of the Duke and Duchess of Gloucester, in March 1980. Originally made for Queen Victoria's first child, the Princess Royal, by the women of Honiton in Devon, it has been worn at Royal christenings ever since.

Prince William Arthur Philip Louis was christened at Buckingham Palace on the 4th August 1982, on the same day as the birthday of his great grandmother Queen Elizabeth the Queen Mother. Two important items of Royal tradition were in evidence. The first was the silver-gilt lily font, brought from Windsor for the occasion, which was designed by Prince Albert and first used on the 10th February 1841 for the christening of the Princess Royal, Queen Victoria's first-born child. It has since held the Holy water that has been sprinkled on the head of many a future monarch, including Princess Elizabeth (the Queen) and Prince Charles. The second was the christening robe itself. This beautiful long lace gown of Honiton lace, with small bows trimming the centre panel, was made for the same Princess Royal by the women of Honiton in Devon. Again, it has become the traditional robe for Royal Family christenings.

The Royal christening robe is, in fact, similar in style to many family christening gowns, most of which date back to, or are copies of, Victorian fashions. One consequence of this is that they will suit either a girl or a boy, and indeed it was only fairly recently that boys and girls wore different styles of clothes during their first year of life. For a time, women would make one of these traditional family robes using material from their wedding dress. Today, this would seem rather extravagant, and a christening robe in traditional style can be made fairly easily without resorting to such vandalism (see page 129). Bonnets, which were once a standard part of the christening outfit – usually a simple lace cap that matched or toned with the robe, such as the one that Lady Rose Windsor wore at her christening – are now much less common.

It often happens these days that children are christened when they are quite a bit older – when they would look quite ridiculous in a traditional christening robe. The Royal Family have not adopted this practice, but many other people have. In this case, an ideal outfit for a small boy would be a shirt and shorts suit, rather similar to the one Prince William wore for the Trooping of the Colour Ceremony in June 1984 (see page 61). A small girl would look good in a pretty outfit, for example the pale blue dress worn by Lady Davina Windsor to the christening of her sister Lady Rose in March 1980 (see page 65). In general, at this age, children can wear anything that would pass for 'Sunday best' (see page 60).

Of course, christenings are a great occasion for mothers to dress up. Depending on the time of year, a silk or lightweight dress, or a smart

Changing styles of Royal christenings. Above; the strict formality of a Victorian christening, with Queen Victoria, still in mourning after the death of Prince Albert, holding the future Edward V111, and the Duke of Windsor and Prince Edward (Edward V11) in formal dress, contrasts with the more relaxed atmosphere of the Queen with Prince Charles (above left), and the Prince and Princess of Wales with Prince William (left).

suit, would look both stylish and appropriate. Christenings usually involve holding the baby for quite a length of time, so make sure that the fabric is not rough, hairy or harsh, and don't wear jewellery on lapels, or lots of long roped-style necklaces or scarves. Since you could be standing for relatively long periods of time, take care to wear comfortable shoes, and don't clutter youself up with too many other accessories such as large handbags and gloves.

Even in the case of the Royal Family, a christening is still a relatively private affair. No Heads of State or other public dignitaries have to be invited, and usually it is only the family and friends who are present. Official photographs are, however, often released. Those of Prince William's christening show him crying indignantly throughout, resisting all attempts of the Queen and Queen Mother to comfort him. Only the reassuring presence of his mother's little finger in his mouth succeeded in calming him down. His father, Prince Charles, was rather more amenable at his own christening, if the official photographs (see previous page) are anything to go by.

As with many aspects of Royal life, christenings have become more relaxed over the years. In Victoria's day, women wore full evening dress and men wore morning suits or military uniforms. Princess Diana, in contrast, wore a simple pink outfit in silk crêpe-de-chine, designed by Belville Sassoon, with a large brimmed pink hat. This dress with matching jacket is very similar in feel to the one worn by the Duchess of Gloucester at her younger daughter's christening (see previous page) and is the sort of thing that could be worn for many different occasions. The Princess of Wales wore a touching addition to her outfit. Around her neck was the diamond heart necklace that Prince Charles gave her on the birth of her first son – in the circumstances, an entirely appropriate choice.

Nursery Style

The nursery is the only room that children can call their own. It deserves a special effort to make it a happy and secure place to be – and even to give it a Royal touch.

Whether it is a converted box room, separate bedroom, or a whole suite with bedroom as well as day room, the nursery is of great importance to a young child. He or she might spend most of the day banging saucepans in the kitchen, pulling books off the book-shelves and generally getting under everbody's feet; but for an after-noon sleep, and for evenings and early mornings, the child needs a room of its own that is comfortable, familiar, and nice to be in. It may be a wrench for the parents to banish their still quite new small baby from their own room to the isolation of a room of its own. But if parents and child are going to weather the trials and tribulations of child rearing and growing up that are ahead of them, the step is essential for them both.

A child's bedroom or nursery has to be both practical and stimu-lating. It is *their* room, and they may well occupy it from babyhood through to their teens. It has to be an adaptable room, and one that can grow with the child. It is a great mistake to design a room so thoroughly around a babe-in-arms that it can't be altered a few months later to accomodate a vigorously crawling and inquisitive infant. Furthermore, unless you have endless money, it is a room that can easily bankrupt you – many parents are at their least sensible when it comes to buying new things for a baby, especially the first. The choice of wall papers, fabrics and endless accessories can be baffling, and the temptation to buy the lot is all too easy to yield to. Careful thought and planning is essential.

In the following pages you will find numerous suggestions for nursery layouts, interior design, equipment, toys and much else, all designed to make growing up more fun for both you and your child. And more regal as well; the designers whose ideas you will find in this chapter are among the select few who have been patronised by, or are in touch with, the Princess of Wales and her family, and Royal children need just the same things from their surroundings as any other child.

Modern nurseries are, of course, much more practical and easy to run than the sprawling, inconveniently placed, ones of past gener-ations. In Queen Victoria's time, the nuseries at Buckingham Palace were so far from the living rooms that Prince Albert used to drag the children through the long passages in baskets. Even more extreme was Princess Alexandra, wife of Edward V11, who had a hole cut in the floor of her children's nursery so that a sleeping child could be lowered and kissed goodnight without being woken – not something to be recommended for most parents. Nurseries have also become rather less grandiose. The Queen and Princess Margaret's nursery consisted of the whole of the top floor of 145 Piccadilly, where they lived until their parents became King and Queen and moved to Buckingham Palace.

Moving house can be quite traumatic for a child, particularly if it involves changing area as well. The presence of familiar things, such as toys, can help to avoid the inevitable disorientation; but the best thing is to recreate as nearly as possible the old nursery in the new

Hand-painted nursery furniture, bought for Prince William's Kensington Palace nursery from Dragons, the specialist nursery boutique in London. Other items in the Royal nursery include a mural of Jungle Book *and other cartoon characters (by artist Simon Barnett) and, in the night nursery, a pine cot with broderie anglaise trimmings occupied first by Prince William and then, in due course, by Prince 'Harry'. There is nothing ponderous or formal in the surroundings of these thoroughly modern Princes.*

house. The Queen was faced with this problem when she had to move Prince Charles and Princess Anne from the accustomed surroundings of Clarence House to the unfamiliar territory of Buckingham Palace. Their former nursery was carefully recreated there – boxes of soldiers, the cuckoo clock and the ten-foot high Tudor doll's house. The fact that the nursery can provide such a sense of security for a child is a measure of its importance: it is a room worth spending time on.

Young Royal children today have far less formal nurseries than their parents or grandparents. There is less fuss and more colour. Prince William's own nursery is bright and cheerful, with modern furniture painted with red and blue rabbits, and this sort of approach tends to be the norm for the modern child. Hand painted furniture is, of course, the most distinctive and individual, but it is expensive. If you don't have the talent to do it yourself (and few of us have), you can always buy transfers, or use stencilling – the technique of applying patterns to a surface through a cardboard or acetate cut-out. You can make them discreet and rather sophisticated, much as Prince William's are, or you can choose them bold, colourful and eye-catching. They can be applied to furniture, fabric (if the design is suitable) or to plain walls. Stencils can be bought ready-made, or you can make your own. They can give a homely, old-world quality (obviously liked by the Princess) which can be particularly appealing on an otherwise rather characterless piece of furniture; and they can be applied to any surface, from floors and ceilings to cots and soft furnishings.

It is worth giving some consideration to other painting techniques for nursery walls. Rag rolling and stippling, for example, are both inexpensive and produce textured surfaces that can be applied to any smooth surface from a small table top or chest of drawers to a whole wall. These techniques are coming back into fashion for drawing rooms as well as nurseries, and they are really quite simple to learn. Rag rolling, for example, merely involves applying a strip of paint in the highlight colour (usually the darker one) on top of the dry base colour, and rolling over it while it is still wet with a twisted lint-free cloth. Probably the most *de luxe* treatment, however, if you have the time for it, is to repaper the room entirely with one of the wide range of colourful and pretty patterned wallpapers that is now available. Always remember that you are decorating the room for a child as well as for yourself. When they get older, children can have a hand in their own nursery decor. Until then, it is up to you to choose something that they enjoy and that suits their emerging personalities.

Finally, do make sure that the room is safe. There should be no low-opening windows that a baby could crawl or fall out of. Keep electric wires and leads carefully hidden, and put special protective covers on sockets. Don't have too many nick-nacks and ornaments in the room, not just because they might get broken but because inquisitive children can pull them on top of themselves and be hurt. Make sure, too, that all pictures and mobiles are securely fixed. And don't let the room get too dark. Young children are easily made to feel insecure or frightened, so have a low night-light as well as the main one. Children need to feel at ease and comfortable in their rooms, not because they spend hours there but so that at bedtimes and during their afternoon sleep they will settle down happily and give both themselves and their parents some peace.

Above left: the nursery at Osborne House, Isle of Wight, in 1875. Queen Victoria brought her children here for fairly frequent holidays. One of the great attractions was the charming cottage in the style of a Swiss chalet erected in the grounds near the sea. The nursery, with several cots and beds, makes few concessions to the natural liveliness of children, although there is a doll's house by the window and a few toys

are scattered on the table. Above right: The Day Nursery, 145 Piccadilly, in 1936. The nursery was painted in green and white and furnished in mahogany, with a glass fronted cabinet in which the Princesses Elizabeth and Margaret displayed their treasures. The night nursery had two white beds decorated with pink roses. It was a grander nursery than most, but not untypical of the nursery style of the times.

Colour

There are no hard and fast rules for nursery colour schemes, but it is certainly not the case that 'anything goes'. Colours are the essence of the room, particularly a nursery. They need to be stimulating and practical, as do the toys and other accessories, but, depending on your taste and the size of the room, you can go for soft pastels, or for strong primaries. Both are suitable for either a boy or a girl. There is still something of a tradition of blue for boys and pink for girls, but if you are decorating before the birth and don't particularly trust the various methods of sex-divination, why not try one of the more unusual combinations of colours, such as lemon and grey. You can always add stronger or deeper colours as the child grows up.

Remember that colours create their own illusions; soft apricots, pinks or greens give a fresh, light and airy feel to a room, while red, navy and white are more powerful and more fun, but they can also sometimes be rather overpowering. The wrong shade of blue, for example, can make a room rather cold and unwelcoming. Try thinking of using all the different shades of a single colour, so that you have a blue room, or a green room – it can make for quite a regal atmosphere. To some extent you need to let the room evolve, in colour as much as in furniture and fittings, so that you create a room that your child will actually enjoy.

Planning and decorating a nursery should be fun rather than hard labour, and it is, after all, one of the more important rooms in your home. Here are some practical tips to consider before you start.

Furniture – especially specialised nursery furniture – can be expensive, so it is important to plan in advance. There is now an enormous amount that you can buy for the nursery. It is no longer the case

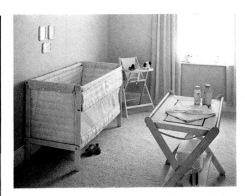

One of Mothercare's newest looks is this lilac-blue small printed fabric, which is used for cots, cribs, changing trolleys and high chairs, giving you a complete coordinated look for the nursery. The cot is particularly interesting in that it is quilted (the fabric can be removed and washed) over a strong wooden frame. There is a mesh inset so that the baby can see what is going on. As they say, "The whole point is that if you buy matching furniture and equipment, it instantly turns a room into a baby's nursery. It is a case of keeping it simple but not too austere, pretty and at the same time practical – and very safe."

that cartoon-character wallpaper and the odd picture on the wall are the only things that distinguish the nursery from an adult bedroom. Mothercare, for example, the leading high street specialists, have now produced a coordinated range of nursery furniture and equipment, in fresh pastel colours which would be suitable for any size of room. Using this sort of furniture, you can keep the walls and curtains fairly plain and still achieve a very pretty and practical nursery. It is also sensible to buy things that have already been coordinated in style and colour, provided they suit the kind of nursery you have in mind, since different pieces of furniture from different sources sometimes don't seem to match very comfortably once you get them home.

To complement specialised nursery furniture, you can buy simple mass-produced wardrobes and chests of drawers, which always look fresh and clean in a child's nursery (and can always be decorated with stencils or transfers). If you don't want to do this, you can paint old wooden furniture, and stripped pine can look equally appealing and attractive. Always be careful, however, when painting in a baby's or young child's room that the paint you are using is non-toxic, particularly with such things as cots which the baby will be in close contact with. Most modern paints are, in fact, safe, but it is not worth taking chances. Always check beforehand.

If you keep all the walls white or plain coloured, use patterned curtains or roller blinds to break the monotony. Experiment with soft furnishings, such as cushions, to inject new colours and patterns. Try mixing several patterns from the same family on different accessories to give the room a 'period', almost Victorian, flavour (see page 84 for a Laura Ashley designed nusery of this sort). Patchwork is another way of adding colourful patterns to children's rooms and a good way of using up scraps of left-over fabric.

Don't put rugs in a child's room, especially on a polished floor. It is so easy for them to fall over and hurt themselves when they are learning to walk, and they get in the way of a crawling baby. Flooring needs to be hard-wearing in a busy nursery. Coil and sisal both answer the description, but they tend to be rather harsh for young feet and skin. Colourful vinyl flooring or cork tiles are highly suitable, or even carpet tiles. If you have bare smooth-surfaced floor boards, try painting them carefully with deck paint.

Storage can be a problem. Even the youngest children seem to have a never ending stream of toys, books and clothes and the space they occupy seems disproportionate for such a small person. Most children like to have them within easy reach, so some form of shelving or large toy box is ideal. Do shop around for the right type of box, whether it is plastic, wooden or cane. It is also important that your child should learn to put away his or her own toys – a form of discipline that many parents neglect by automatically doing it themselves. It will be interesting to see whether Prince William is sent to the Montessori nursery school which, rumour has it, is favoured by the Princess of Wales. One of the rules is that all children have to clear away their own toys when they have finished playing with them.

If the purchase of a special wardrobe for the nursery seems unduly extravagant, why not cover shelving and hanging space with a large, colourful printed roller blind, blending it in with the rest of the colour scheme, or making a distinctive feature of it?

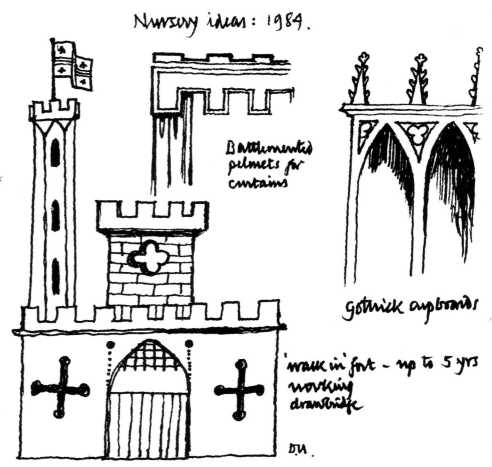

Nursery ideas: 1984.

Battlemented pelmets for curtains

gothick cupboards

'walk in' fort - up to 5 yrs working drawbridge

D.H.

This idea for a theme nursery was sketched out for us by David Hicks, one of Britain's leading interior designers as well as father of three children. "All boys love playing at soldiers." He says." My idea here is very similar to the one I used in my son's room." The basic colours can be khaki, using a general's scarlet as a highlighter – so you could have cushions in khaki piped in scarlet. The rest of the room can follow a military theme too: battlement pelmets for the curtains; and cupboards or wardrobes can be livened up by using using panels of plywood as a fascia to achieve a sort of 'gothic' effect. If you have a do-it-yourself minded husband, you could even have a walk-in fort (complete with a drawbridge), which could provide hours of entertainment for children under five, as well as useful storage space for toys.

Nursery Themes

Once your child has grown up a bit, you can have a great deal of fun with a nursery. Try adopting a single strong theme. David Hicks, one of Britain's leading interior designers, has given an example (see above) using a military theme for a small boy's nursery. David Hicks has had plenty of experience of nurseries, being himself the father of three children (one of whom, India, was a bridesmaid to the Prince and Princess of Wales). When designing any room, he always applies the same 'Hicks rule' – "To transform a room in seconds, use lighting, and in hours use colour. For instance, a room can be given a different atmosphere instantly by the use of a coloured lamp, rather similar to the type that you can easily buy in Habitat. And with a little more effort, a girl's pink bedroom can be made into a boy's by simply repainting. All you need, again, is a do-it-yourself husband." His other advice is to invest in a good sofa bed. "They can be so useful, not only for putting up your children's friends, but other relatives too." Anyone who has children will know that they soon want their friends to stay (particularly if they have a walk-in fort).

Although they may not be so active, babies and very young children too need plenty of stimulation, particularly at the stage when they are just beginning to take an interest in the world around them. There must be lots of points of interest. Mobiles and friezes are ideal. They are not expensive, and come in a huge variety of shapes, designs and sizes. Young babies will often lie and watch a mobile for hours in wonder and amazement, and for older children they can be a great comfort as they go to sleep. Like many other things, mobiles are easy to make, using materials lying around the home – bits from an old wooden jigsaw puzzle, or old pieces of wool made into pom-poms by winding wool around two pieces of circular cardboard.

Friezes too are a good way of creating colour and interest. There are many different types, for children of all ages. They make ideal coverings for plain walls. But don't make the mistake of putting them too high up where the baby or child can't see them. You can make your own frieze by cutting up old birthday or Christmas cards, particularly colourful children's ones. Cards like these can also be handy for lining the sides of a pram, where the baby lies otherwise staring at nothing. A card or small paper picture can keep eager young eyes interested. Don't attach anything that might hurt or fall onto a baby and alarm it.

A period nursery

The name of Laura Ashley has become synonymous with a style of pretty and traditional fashion, both in women's and children's clothes and in interior decoration. The Princess of Wales is known to be among their customers. The two nurseries featured here (see facing page and overleaf) have a strong Victorian period flavour, very much in keeping with Laura Ashley's general style, but both are still entirely appropriate for a modern home as well as an old one. The one on the facing page is a very simple room, showing how easy it is to create an attractive nursery for a new-born baby. The crib is covered in a tiny floral patterned fabric – which would work just as well on a Moses basket. A good idea is to shop around second hand shops (or even relative's attics) to find an old crib that can be renovated in this way. Of course, this will in turn be replaced by a cot, and then a bed, using the same or similar patterned fabric for bed coverings and linen so that the whole room will not need complete redecoration. The result is a room that is fresh, clean and relaxing, and can be adapted for children of almost any age, from young babies upwards.

To create this type of nursery you need to coordinate carefully, choosing a very positive colour scheme and then incorporating different patterns and prints that work together. The nursery shown opposite is a relatively simple example; but it is quite possible to mix together a number of different patterns and fabrics (see overleaf). This can be very successful, Laura Ashley explain, "providing all the patterns marry together rather than fighting each other: they don't have to match strictly, but need to coordinate and colour link. We have started out by working on a colour scheme. This one, for example, is pink, green and white, using this combination in a large floral design for the walls and mixing three fabrics – print and plain, in all three colours – for the window decoration. For the other soft furnishings, stick to fabrics in either pink/white or green/white. It is better to use a bolder print for the walls, keeping smaller prints to complement it." To give a child's bedroom a very cosy, secure feeling, Laura Ashley suggest covering the ceiling in a small-printed wall paper (definitely not a large print). This is a good way of lowering a room that has a very

No nursery is complete without toys. This Laura Ashley nursery is complete with the traditional rocking horse, and a doll's house and pram, all of which suit the 'period' style of the room. They are also perennial children's favourites.

high ceiling, or of giving an 'attic' effect to a room. Windows too can be made to look interesting if you feel like a change from traditional curtains. You can keep the room light and airy by using net or lace curtains, and than have a roller blind (which you can make up cheaply from a kit) behind them. For special effect, a length of fabric can be used to dress the pelmets. Borders too can be used to finish off the wallpaper or to break up an expanse of plain wall.

If you are really trying to create a special room for your child, remember to pay particular attention to detail. Such simple things as a patchwork quilt or bedspread can make a lot of difference to a room. A trunk to store toys in can be covered. It just takes a little extra thought and a bit of imagination to transform a room into a very attractive nursery. It is less expensive than you might expect, and Laura Ashley show very effectively how it can be done.

Laura Ashley has designed here a Victorian style nursery which, as is characteristic of all her firm's work, is very pretty and has lots of charm. The device of mixing several prints together makes the room cosy while leaving the design very practical. As the drawing suggests, there is no need to restrict the theme to wallpaper and curtains; use it

for the soft furnishings as well. There are also some highly practical ideas. For instance, the wall pocket hanger and pannier could be used either for baby things – creams, talcum powder, nappies and pins – or for an older child's cherished bits and pieces. The chest of drawers surface can double up as a changing surface – to keep the Victorian

theme practical it would be best to have whitewood funiture rather than the heavy Victorian kind, again using painting or stencils to coordinate it with the rest of the decor. Bedlinen too can be incorporated into the general scheme of things; for a cot or small bed, you can easily make sheets, pillowcases and even duvet covers yourself from matching

fabric, and they suit this style of nursery extremely well. And simply because you are planning on a Victorian style nursery, it doesn't mean that you have to put up with Victorian standards of discomfort and impracticality. Why not have a bed with drawers underneath, for example, so that there is extra storage space for clothes, linen or even toys.

The Dragon's nursery

Dragons is the name of one of London's leading specialist nursery shops, famous for its furnture and for its murals. Owned and run by Rosy Fisher, the shop has been patronised by several members of the Royal Family, including the Duchess of Gloucester and Princess Diana. It was Dragons who supplied the furniture for Prince William's nursery at Kensington Palace (see page 76) and William's grandfather, Earl Spencer, has bought things there for all his grandchildren.

Dragons provide a way of 'customising' the nursery. Their hand-painted furniture and murals are all done to suit your own individual taste. As Rosy Fisher explains: "It is a way of giving a room a very personal touch, which means that a child can feel that it's somewhere very special." Such things provide a stimulus to the imagination. A young child lying gazing at a familiar picture, for example a scene from the *Wind in the Willows* (see below) will identify with it, relax and become part of the story, entering for a while a little fantasy world. Prince William has a scene from *The Jungle Book* painted on the wall of his nursery, introducing him to Rudyard Kipling's ever-popular children's characters.

Murals can completely change the feel of a room. A country scene painted on the wall of an urban nursery can bring in a breath of rural freshness; and in a rather cold-looking or sparsely furnished room, a cosy scene, such as the interior of a cottage, painted on the ceiling as

Above: on a windowless wall, even a pretend window in the form of a mural can give the illusion of space and light, and of beautiful scenery outside. This design would be ideal for small rooms or in city houses and appartments. Right: a scene from the Wind in the Willows, *Kenneth Graham's masterpiece for children. Both painted for Dragons by Anna de Polnay.*

A nursery is transformed. The cottage scene covers walls and ceiling, giving the room an entirely different atmosphere.

well as the walls, can change the atmosphere completely. One point to remember is not to clutter up the room; let the mural speak for itself. Hand-painted murals are, of course, expensive – although many parents would consider them money well-spent. So what happens when you move house? Rosy Fisher's own advice is to have the mural painted on a good medium density fibre board which can be fixed carefully to the wall and then removed when the time comes.

A rather less drastic way of personalising the nursery is to use hand-painted furniture. As well as familiar nursery characters, you could add your child's name as part of the decoration. You can transform a simple bedhead or cot (for young babies always check that you are using lead-free paint) by painting something cheerful on it. Often this can be done by stencilling, although Dragons themselves never do this – one of their artists personally handpaints the entire design to the customer's specifications. Follow the design through to the wall, which gives an interesting *trompe l'oeil* effect; as Rosy Fisher says, "This can be particularly effective with a simple motif, such as a row of cats painted onto the bedhead and wall".

Left: Beatrix Potter's appeal endures from generation to generation. Her nursery characters also attract children from when they are very young until they are almost in their teens. Beatrix Potter furniture decorations or murals would suit a child from newborn to nine or ten years old. Right: painted furniture, including headboards and chests of drawers, provides an excellent way of personalising a room. Again, this would suit a baby as well as a much older child. Below left: never feel that a nursery has to be alien to the rest of the house. As here, you can link colours and patterns together in a way which would blend with other rooms. Below right: simple hand-painted designs on rather old fashioned cottage style furniture can look delightful. Note how the details match or tone with the wall covering.

A cheerful nursery

Linda Beard, one of England's leading fabric designers, had one major consideration in mind when she designed this nursery. "I think nurseries should be like children", she says. "They should grow. By that, I mean that the room can be suitable for a baby, but then, with minor adaptations, it should be ideal for a toddler and a slightly older child." In this design, for example, the desk-style table and chair could have doubled up previously as a changing surface for the baby and a chair for mother. The wall pocket board could have held creams and talcum powder instead of toys.

The essence of Linda's nursery is the coordination of prints and colours so that the rooms are cheerful and bright. "Don't be afraid of using two different patterned prints in the same room, providing that they are sensibly balanced. Keep all the prints in the same colourway, or otherwise they could clash terribly." she advises. Linda has demonstrated how this can be done by ensuring that both prints – one bold and used for the duvet and bed linen, the other small and used for the blind, curtains, wardrobe and cot – are in the same colours. With so much going on in the room, the walls have plain white, but the woodwork has been picked out in primary colours to match the prints.

The other familiar problem in children's rooms is storage. The idea in this design is to have plenty of toys on display, keeping them in a shelving unit that could be adapted and made up in a number of different ways. Toys are often very decorative in themselves, and obviously appropriate in a child's room, and they give the room a very personal atmosphere. When the shelves are required for more serious matters such as books, stamp collections or photographs of pop stars, some at least of the toys can be relegated to the storage space beneath the window seat. For an older child, the seat itself forms a private niche in which to sit and read, or simply daydream. This is thus a practical and cheerful room, suitable for almost any type of house, and one that it would be fun to grow up in.

A bright and cheerful nursery for a boy or girl of almost any age, from a small baby upwards. Linda Beard, who designed this nursery, has used coordinating wall paper, fabrics and bedlinen in a style called Topaz, from her Dolly Mixture range. (This together with the Men Only range, which she also designs, are all available through Colorall). This is an idea that can easily be adapted to suit many different rooms of widely differing shapes and sizes. For example, the wall paper used on the wardrobe door could be used in between the ceiling eves or, of course, on the walls itself.

The suggestions here are easy enough to incorporate into an existing nursery, but, at the same time, they could give it a complete face-lift.

Rooms for all ages

Comfort, says Tricia Guild, "is the first and foremost thing people should be thinking of when they furnish any part of their home". Tricia Guild, head of Designers Guild, is one of the most successful young designers in Britain today. With her team of young associates, she has had a great influence on the materials that we now buy to furnish our homes, whether we shop at do-it-yourself stores or designer shops. Designers Guild is also among the establishments patronised by Royalty, from many countries, choosing fabrics and wallpapers from their range to furnish their own homes.

The basic Designers Guild philosophy is simple. They feel that, whatever room you are decorating, and however fashionable you want it to be, it should not become out of date within a mere two or three years. Fashions do change in interior design, just as they do with clothes – although, fortunately, the turnover is rather slower. Nor should the fashion element make the room difficult to inhabit. As they say, "it is pointless having a beautiful room which you are afraid to live in". With these principles in mind, Designers Guild have produced three exclusive designs for three styles of nursery, each taking a different theme. One is very much for a young girl, a 'fairytale' nursery with a touch of magic; another is for children to share, whether they are babies, toddlers or sixteen-year old teenagers; and a third is for a room that could be used equally as a nursery or as an adult bedroom.

"A nursery can be one of the most exciting rooms in the house, full of imagination with a touch of fantasy. You can be slightly extravagant with the design, but without being too serious ." Their four-poster bedroom setting, for example, has a slightly fantastic, not to say regal, air to it, but it is practical nevertheless. It would certainly delight any little girl, and who knows what dreams would be dreamed in it?

Colour is obviously as important for a nursery as it is for any other room – possibly even more so. This is one good reason, as Designers Guild suggest, why it doesn't make sense to rush into complete redecoration before your child is born. "Instead of completely finishing the nursery or bedroom before the baby arrives, it may well be better to do it up in such a way that the final details can be left until later. That way, you can build and design the rest of the room around your child, adapting the design and bringing out the colours and features that suit him or her best." People still often stick to the old fashioned belief in blue for boys and pink for girls; but there is no rule to say that you should. In fact, it makes life easier, particularly if you are decorating before the birth, if you find alternatives. In fact, with careful coordination, you can provide a room with lots of colour and pattern, in such variety that no single colour dominates. The design on page 95 is a very effective demonstration of this. And the functional aspects of the nursery can be made to combine with entertainment as well as colour: foam cubes and blocks, for example, can be covered in coordinated colours and used not just for seating but for building with or simply for playing around (see opposite). Finally, a nursery needs to grow with your children. No-one wants to be redecorating all the time. As Tricia Guild says, "a room should not be too static. It needs to be added to in order to grow."

Nursery Style

This room is in predominantly pink, blue and grey fabrics (Triangel, from Designers Guild's Natural Classics range). Two bed sofas with ample cushions make it an ideal setting for a dayroom or nursery for one or two children from toddler-age upwards. If used as a dayroom, it could easily double up as a room for unexpected visitors. Fun foam building blocks covered in the blue, pink and green fabrics give the children the opportunity to create their own den or hideaway, (a game much-loved by all children), to stack them as an early exercise in sculpture or to jump up and down on them. Roman blinds with contrasting colour battens complete a nursery that has the style and the flexibility to grow in pace with its occupants.

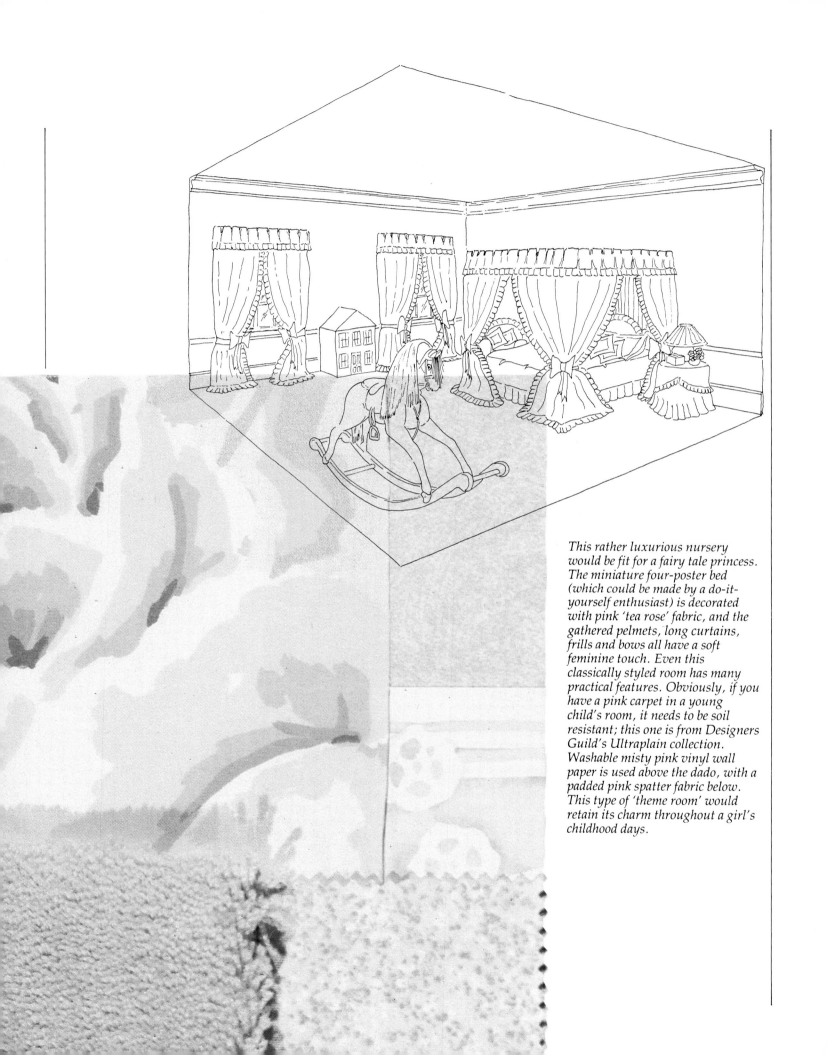

This rather luxurious nursery would be fit for a fairy tale princess. The miniature four-poster bed (which could be made by a do-it-yourself enthusiast) is decorated with pink 'tea rose' fabric, and the gathered pelmets, long curtains, frills and bows all have a soft feminine touch. Even this classically styled room has many practical features. Obviously, if you have a pink carpet in a young child's room, it needs to be soil resistant; this one is from Designers Guild's Ultraplain collection. Washable misty pink vinyl wall paper is used above the dado, with a padded pink spatter fabric below. This type of 'theme room' would retain its charm throughout a girl's childhood days.

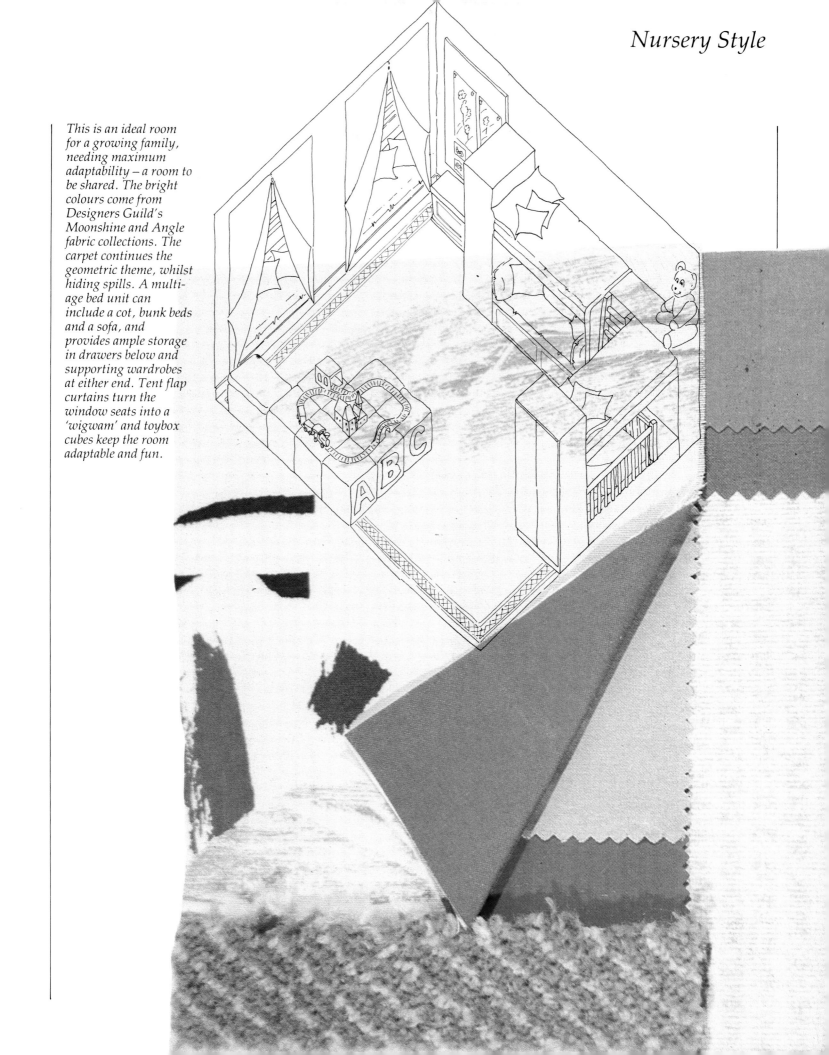

This is an ideal room for a growing family, needing maximum adaptability – a room to be shared. The bright colours come from Designers Guild's Moonshine and Angle fabric collections. The carpet continues the geometric theme, whilst hiding spills. A multi-age bed unit can include a cot, bunk beds and a sofa, and provides ample storage in drawers below and supporting wardrobes at either end. Tent flap curtains turn the window seats into a 'wigwam' and toybox cubes keep the room adaptable and fun.

Cribs, cradles and cots

Babies spend most of the first few months of their lives fast asleep, so it is not surprising that their sleeping arrangements have always received a lot of attention. Ornate cribs and cradles, with bodywork that would have done credit to a nobleman's coach, are uncommon nowadays. As elsewhere, the trend is towards simple, practical, cheap and cheerful. Good examples of the old fashioned cradle may be delightful – no baby can fail to look enchanting in one – but they are certainly expensive. Considering how short a time it will be occupied, most parents-to-be would think twice before rushing out to buy one.

Nevertheless, if you are determined to provide your new baby with nothing but the best, and will brook no argument, then go ahead. A well made cradle will last at least a lifetime: it can be lent to relatives and friends, and passed on to subsequent generations. A fine cradle soon becomes an heirloom of great sentimental value. This is very much in accordance with Royal practice. The Princess of Wales, for example, spent the first six months of her life in the Althorp family cradle - complete with lace curtains fringed with broderie anglaise.

Even if you don't want to go to these lengths, there is a great deal to be said for looking around antique or junk shops to find a plain wooden or cane cradle and then making a fabric trimming for it yourself. This will certainly be cheaper than a shop bought model, and can look very charming (see page 83 for an example). You can also buy less extravagantly decorated cribs, if these are more your style, such as the wooden cradle that swings and has its own drape. The other fashionable alternative is the Moses basket – a large wickerwork basket, suitable only for very young babies, but in which they not only sleep but can also be carried around. They can be bought already lined with plain or quilted fabric, mostly in a small print, but you can, if you prefer, buy a plain basket and line it yourself. Make sure the fabric is washable. It is worth shopping around for Moses baskets, since prices can vary enormously. Carry cots, too, have long been considered an ideal way of transporting a baby, particularly for car journeys since they can be securely strapped in. These days they are rarely bought separately but incorporated in a pram – a carry cot on wheels.

As the baby grows up, it usually moves into a cot, before sleeping in an unguarded bed. These come in a wide variety of designs, from modern to traditional, usually white and wooden although metal and plastic are also used. Some have drawers underneath, and others can be converted into a bed by removing the sides. One point worth considering is the depth of the cot – one with an adjustable mattress height can be very useful and can save you a lot of unnecessary bending and stooping when the baby is young. Plain cots, or old and slightly battered ones, can be made a bit more special by stencilling nursery characters onto the front and back, or by decorating them with a cot bumper made from a pretty print or broderie anglaise.

An important aspect of all cribs, cradles and cots, whether modern or traditional, portable or fixed, is accessories. Children and babies like and need visual stimulation: mobiles or cot toys are almost essential – indeed many young children won't sleep without their favourite bedtime toy beside them, and cheerful and familiar objects are always important in giving a child a sense of comfort and security.

Left: a portrait of Princess Alice, daughter of Queen Victoria, being guarded in her ornate cradle by Dandie the terrier. Sir Edwin Landseer was smuggled into the nursery to paint it as a surprise for the Queen. Below left: Princess Alice's youngest sister Princess Beatrice, in May 1875 aged three weeks, graces a different but certainly no less elaborate crib. Below right: Princess Elizabeth and Princess Margaret with some of their toys and the crib formerly used by them both at the Exhibition of Historic and Royal Treasures assembled in Princess Elizabeth's room at 145 Piccadilly in May 1939.

Carriages, prams and buggies

Lady Diana Spencer at Park House, Sandringham in a 'baby perambulator' of the old-fashioned but still popular sort.

Prince William in a thoroughly modern baby buggy on an outing in the Park in July 1983.

The heavy, gleaming perambulator, a true Rolls Royce among baby carriages, is forever associated with the British aristocracy. Immaculately upholstered, generously sprung, and effortlessly driven by a nanny in a crisp starched uniform, it provided a smooth and bump-free introduction to the world for the children of the rich and the Royal. The Queen put her children in them, as, occasionally, the Princess of Wales has done with hers. Indeed, one of Prince Charles's earliest memories is of peeping out of a huge pram – in fact the Queen's old one, which she had had refurbished for him. Often manufactured by the firm of Silver Cross, these prams have stayed in vogue for many years. Even today, when more practical, versatile and lightweight baby carriages are available, many families still prefer the old fashioned perambulator. They are investments: they can

usually be returned to the manufacturers for servicing and renovation as often as you like, so that they can be used for several children in the family, as well as for their children in time to come. The manufacturers themselves say that this practice is on the increase, so no doubt many parents are rediscovering the virtues of the traditional family pram.

One thing that does make these prams rather impractical (apart from their cost) is their size. With the trend for people to live in smaller houses and in flats and appartments, large prams become very cumbersome, as well as being difficult to manoeuvre. This is where the smaller and lighter modern pram comes into its own. These carry-cot style prams and collapsible buggies are much more appropriate for today's lifestyle. They have even been adopted by the Royal family,

and both Princess Anne and the Princess of Wales have used them on occasion. Like others of their generation, the modern Royal child spends more of his or her time in a pushchair, or rather a buggy, than in a full scale pram. For working mothers, and those living in towns, they have become more or less indispensible. They are safe and practical; they fold up easily and weigh very little; and they are, of course, ideal for travelling, whether in a car, or in trains and buses. They can be quite basic in style, or they can be very luxurious, depending on what your needs are and how much you want to spend. Many are equipped with hoods, aprons, feeding and play trays, and parasols. Some recent models are even capable of carrying a new-born baby, and for those families with two small children or with twins, the double buggy is likely to be an essential.

Above: an appropriate if over-sized baby carriage for Charles and Anne for celebrations after the Coronation in June 1953. Child-size versions for George VI aged two (right) and Prince Albert Victor of Wales (below) seem almost practical.

Toys

Toys somehow epitomise childhood. They are an essential aspect of growing up. To a child, almost anything is a toy. From their very first rattle or teething ring, babies are beginning to explore and to familiarise themselves with the world around them. As they grow older, toys are essential to keep them amused and to continue the process of learning, whether they are educational or simply widening the child's experience of everyday things. Eventually toys grade into hobbies; they become an introduction to the adult world.

Some of the best toys are those that have been passed down from one generation to another. No doubt Royal children, like many others, have computer games, Action Man and Sindy dolls in their collections. But they also have a rich store of historic toys to play with. Peter Phillips, for example, often plays with a toy horse, complete with bridle and saddle, which used to belong to Prince Charles, and which the Queen keeps at Buckingham Palace – in the Royal Family, as elsewhere, grandmother keeps her own children's old toys for her grandchildren to play with.

Parts of the Royal toy collection are famous, and there have been various exhibitions of them over the years. There are more than 500 dolls – an historic collection in its own right – as well as numerous doll's houses and clothes. Queen Elizabeth's favourites would have seemed to be toy horses rather than dolls, and she was given them endlessly. In the end she amassed more than thirty of them. It was also little Princess Elizabeth who was given the miniature house *Y Bwthyn Bach to Gelt* (The Little Cottage with the Straw Foot), by the people of Wales.

The Queen's first toy was an ivory handled rattle – still a favourite gift for a new-born baby (and an ideal

Above right: Princess Elizabeth and Princess Margaret in 1933, with one example of the numerous toy horses they collected. Below right: Prince Charles plays with his horse and carriage in Clarence House garden in April 1951.

Top: Prince Charles at Balmoral in 1952 clearly enjoyed his motor car as much as any child of his age. No doubt Prince William will soon be on the road. Above: Prince Charles rolls the lawns of Clarence House — miniature gardening tools are long-time Royal favourites. Right: Prince Andrew and friend.

christening present) – which was given to her by Queen Mary. Prince William was given a silver rattle by the people of Tetbury, the small Cotswold town close to Highgrove, the Prince and Princess's home in Gloucestershire. It is likely that one of Prince Harry's first presents was a Paddington Bear. Prince William was given one when he left St Mary's, Paddington, by members of the staff of the Lindo Wing, and it has become something of a tradition they are given to all Royal babies when they leave the hospital. And, of course, all Royal children have had their share of cuddly stuffed animals.

In fact, it would be a mistake to think that Royal children always played with exquisite, highly expensive toys. For the most part, their nurseries are lined with very much the sort of toys and books that you might find anywhere. Prince Charles' favourite toy as a toddler was 'Jumbo', an elephant on wheels, who helped the young Prince, as he probably did so many other small children of the time, in learning to walk. Princess Margaret was given a collection of farm animals from Woolworths for her first birthday present. And the books – fairy tales, Dr Doolittle, Beatrix Potter, Peter Pan, would also be familiar to children everywhere. Like so many girl's of her age, the Queen was noted for her fondness for horsey books. As in any other family, not every present is a complete success. Prince Philip presented Prince Charles and Princess Anne with a pair of boxing gloves, but, unfortunately, they had to be taken away after Princess Anne very nearly knocked Charles out.

Where Royal children differ very considerably from their contemporaries is in the volume of presents they receive from unknown well-wishers. The birth of a Royal baby can call forth an absolute deluge. Prince William received large quantities: few of them were as beautiful as the book of nursery rhymes made entirely of lace, which it took the lace-makers of Beer in Devon ten thousand hours to make. Royal tours can also lead to a flood of gifts, whether from ordinary people or from statesmen and politicians. In Australia, the Prince and Princess of Wales received numerous gifts on behalf of Prince William, ranging from fire engines to Koala bears. There are times when this can get out of hand. When the Queen's parents made their own tour of Australia shortly after Princess Elizabeth was born, they were presented with three tons of toys for her (later distributed among the under-privileged children of Durham). In her turn, the Queen was presented with a crocodile for Prince Andrew when she visited a village in Gambia in 1961. Sir Martin Charteris, the Queen's Private Secretary at the time, was obliged to keep it in his bath for the rest of the tour. And when Prince Charles was seven, he was given a child-sized working model of a muck-shifter by workmen who were digging up the road outside Buckingham Palace. Prince Charles, like any small boy would have loved it; but would his mother have felt the same?

Above: Princess Elizabeth outside Y Bwthyn Bach To Gwelt (The Little Cottage with the Straw Foot), a gift to the Princess in 1931, when she was six years old, from the people of Wales. The cottage, which is a sort of superior 'wendy house' was erected in the grounds of Windsor Great Park and has remained a favourite of Royal children ever since. Three year old Peter Phillips made full use of it (left) pouring pretend tea in the miniature kitchen.

Facing page. Familiar toys for today's Royal child; tried and trusted favourites may well give greater pleasure than more elaborate (and expensive) ones would do. Above left: father and son at Kensington Palace. Above right: Prince William enjoys that most familiar of toys, a garden swing, on official photo call on his second birthday. Below: Lord Frederick Windsor, with his mother Princess Michael of Kent on his first birthday receives one of the best of presents for a mobile small child: a traditional wooden tricycle.

The nanny

The nanny has been a constant figure in the upbringing of Royal children. Often their role has been a vital one. With parents committed to a long round of State occasions, overseas tours and other cares of office, the nanny has often been the most important influence during the formative early years. We are today rather more aware of how sensitive children are during their first few years, and parents now are less ready to leave the job entirely to a nanny. It is significant that Princess Diana and Prince Charles took Prince William with them during their triumphant tours of Australia and New Zealand in 1983. However good the nanny, there is no real substitute for the mother, as the Princess has recognised.

This is not to say that nannies are a bad thing. A good one is an excellent supplement to a mother, and allows her the freedom of action that modern women claim as their right. It is ironic that nannies, once the preserve of the wealthy, are much more common in these more egalitarian times than they used to be. The reason is, of course, that so many mothers these days go out to work. One consequence of this is that the old image of the nanny – a rather stern, starched and uniformed figure – is fading fast. There are still, of course, the professionally trained nannies who have attended private colleges like England's Norland Institute (which has always professed to produce the cream of this profession). But alongside them are many young girls, with nursing experience, who are anything but staid and old fashioned.

Choosing a nanny, as any mother knows, is far too important to be taken lightly. Children need care as well as love and intellectual stimulation; personality is as important as professional competence. Parents will always make their own choice in the question of amateur versus professional, but whichever they choose, there are plenty of honourable Royal precedents. The Queen never looked for formally trained nannies; she wanted someone with a kind nature who loved children, as did her own mother before her. The Queen's first nanny was Mrs Knight – a no-nonsense family retainer, who never took holidays or days off. Brought in to assist her as under-nanny was Margaret MacDonald (Bobo) who came from Scotland, and was a huge success. She has remained in the Queen's service ever since, becoming one of her most trusted friends and confidantes. Another Royal favourite is Mabel Anderson, who got the job of under-nanny to nurse Lightbody by advertising in the *Lady* (still the best magazine for such things). Mabel Anderson was totally devoted to her charges – she told Anne and Charles magical stories, invented wonderfully imaginative games and never shouted or spanked them, but she managed to be firm at the same time. She went on to look after Andrew and Edward, and when Princess Anne had her first baby, Peter, she went to look after him. The Princess of Wales herself has chosen a nanny, Barbara Barnes, with no formal training, but she comes with the best of recommendations (and word of mouth is one of the best ways of finding a nanny). Colin and Lady Anne Tennant, with whom she spent many years said of her "she is exceptionally firm, with a great sense of humour. The children absolutely adore her". Clearly, young Prince William and little Prince Harry are in the best of hands.

Dressmaking Patterns

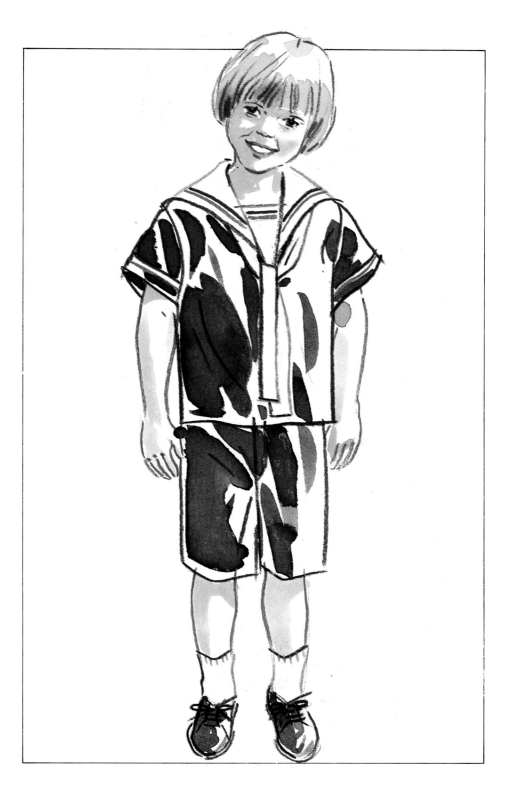

Dressmaking should be a less expensive way of wearing good quality clothes, not a cheap way of making poor ones. Home dress-made clothes can look every bit as good as those you buy from a shop providing that you do the job well – set yourself high standards. Well made clothes that you have sewn or knitted yourself can be a source of deserved satisfaction.

Firstly, it makes sense to buy good fabrics: silk, Viyella, fine wools, and cottons are all hard wearing as well as good looking fabrics. Some modern blended fabrics are also excellent. It doesn't take any longer to sew in a fine cloth than it does in an inferior one, and the inferior one probably won't suit the pattern you are making anyway. Any professional dressmaker will tell you that the best time to buy such fabrics is during the sales, when you can often snap up beautiful remnants, discount lines or even current stock that is moving rather slowly out of the shop. Avoid gimmicky prints, or buy them in cheaper fabric mixes and blends – by their very nature, they tend to date more quickly than the timeless classic patterns such as checks and spots, and the good quality plain fabrics.

Even if you have spent all your money on a good quality main fabric for your pattern, it is still worth finding a bit more for the trimmings. As with all clothes, you need to pay attention to such details as buttons, braids, collars and so on. It is amazing how easy it is to make an otherwise very nice dress look cheap by using the wrong type of buttons. Search out junk shops and antique markets for second-hand lace collars or hand-painted buttons, as well as keeping a close eye on your local haberdashery counter. If you dressmake regularly, it is worth buying these things when you see them and keeping them for future use.

Everyone sews slightly differently, and experience is the only safeguard against mistakes. Nevertheles, it is worth taking a tip from the experts, and our dressmaker has a few for you to follow.

It is a lot easier to overcast or finish edges before you start making up, in other words, while the piece is still flat. And it may seem rather ridiculous, but many top dressmakers say that they spend more time working out the pattern and the correct fittings before they start sewing than they do in the actual making up. Remember that it is absolutely essential to iron at every single stage. All professional dressmakers know that you must keep the iron and ironing board up while you are sewing.

All the patterns in this book are graded to standard size for adults and children, but, as we all know, human beings are anything but standard. So do check actual pattern measurements against your own, or those of your child, before you cut into your fabric. Then adjust accordingly if necessary. Mistakes at this stage can be very expensive. All the cutting out plans are given on a grid in which each square represents 5cm. If you are working in imperial units (yards and inches), this can be taken accurately as a square of 2 inches.

Finally, always choose the right fabric for the pattern, or the look of your outfit might be ruined, no matter how fantastic the design.

Baby's romper suit

Mainly worn by baby boys, the romper suit can look delightful. Choose an appropriate colour, or even a very soft, light patterned fabric. Silk crêpe de chine is the traditional fabric for this suit, and is the one we have used here. However, a polyester crêpe de chine or cotton, providing it is not too stiff, would work just as well. It is important when making baby clothes to make sure that there is plenty of room. They should be in no way tight or restricting. If you are making up before the birth (or as a present) – which is highly likely since you are not likely to have the time to do it once the baby has arrived – it is wise to opt for a larger rather than a smaller size. The baby will grow into it anyway, and it's a shame to see your hard work discarded at too early a stage.

Size: to fit up to a six-month old baby.

Materials: 80cm/⅞yd of 90cm/36in wide fabric.
Lightweight Supershape Iron-On Vilene.
5 6mm/¼in buttons.
1 press stud.
Approximately 15cm/6in of lightweight popper tape.
Shirring elastic.
80cm/⅞yd of 5mm/3⁄16in elastic.
Matching thread.

Cutting out: follow the graph pattern to make a paper pattern using dressmakers' 5cm/2in squared pattern paper. Follow cutting layout to cut out romper. Cut a strip of bias fabric for neck binding 25mm/1in wide by approximately 35cm/14in long, where marked. Cut two strips of Vilene 2.5cm x 30.5cm/1in x 12in for romper back self-facing, and two strips 2.5cm x 8cm/1in x 3⅛in for yoke back self-facing.

Special note: follow the hints on sewing silk listed with the christening robe instructions (page 130). See the special note on machine smocking for the girl's spotted Viyella smocked dress (page 120).

Seam allowances of 15mm/⅝in are included in the pattern, except at neck edge, where it is 6mm/¼in.

Making up
Run two rows of gathering stitches 15mm/⅝in and 10mm/⅜in from top edge of romper front and backs, starting and stopping 15mm/⅝in in from side edges, and 25mm/1in in from centre back edges. Machine smock romper front as for girl's spotted Viyella smocked dress, with first row 1cm/⅜in below lower row of gathering stitches, and second and third rows each 1cm/⅜in below previous row. Draw up elastic *gently* until front measures the same as lower edge of yoke front: secure all ends very firmly.

Pin and stitch upper edge of romper front to lower edge of yoke front, right sides facing, drawing up gathering threads evenly. Stitch again 6mm/¼in inside first stitching and trim seam allowances close to second stitching: zig-zag these edges together and press seam towards yoke.

Fuse strips of Vilene to wrong side of romper back self-facings and yoke back self-facings, centring between seamlines at top and bottom.

Pin and stitch upper edge of romper backs to lower edge of yoke backs, right sides facing, drawing up gathering threads evenly. Stitch again 6mm/¼in inside first stitching and trim seam allowances close to second stitching: zig-zag these edges together and press seam towards yoke.

Press back self-facings to wrong side along foldline and tack together at top and lower edges: catch-stitch yoke seam allowances together.

Pin and stitch front yoke to back yokes at shoulders, right sides facing: trim seam allowances to 6mm/¼in and zig-zag together, press towards back.

Stay-stitch neck edge by stitching with small stitches just inside the 6mm seamline. Press under 6mm/¼in on each long edge of neck binding and allow to cool completely. Use to bind neck edge, stretching slightly as you go and turning under ends neatly at centre back edges.

Make buttonholes in left back opening, having one 1cm/⅜in below neck binding, one 1cm/⅜in above yoke seam, and the others at 7.5cm/3in intervals below that, all starting 6mm/¼in in from edge.

Run two rows of gathering stitches 15mm/⅝in and 10mm/⅜in from raw edge of sleevehead inbetween notches. Pin and stitch sleeveheads to armholes, right sides facing, matching notches, shoulders and sides, pulling up gathering threads evenly. Stitch again 6mm/¼in inside first stitching and trim seam allowances close to second stitching: zig-zag together and press towards sleeve.

Pin and stitch side and sleeve seams in one continuous movement, right sides facing: trim seam allowances to 6mm/¼in and zig-zag together. Press towards backs.

Press under 5mm/3⁄16in along lower edge of sleeves, then 10mm/⅜in, and stitch close to first fold, leaving a gap at underarm to insert elastic. Cut two lengths of elastic the same measurement as child's upper arm and slot through gap in hem. Stitch ends together securely and stitch up gap in hem.

Press under 5mm/3⁄16in along lower edge of rompers, then 10mm/⅜in, and stitch a casing for elastic inbetween notches: cut two lengths of elastic 16cm/6¼in each and slot through casing, extending ends either side of notches by 6mm/¼in: stitch ends securely. Stitch remaining hem.

Lap left back 2cm/¾in over right back and tack together at lower edge Press lower back 1cm/⅜in to right side and lower front 1cm/⅜in to wrong side. Using a zipper foot, stitch ball section of popper tape to lower front over raw edge: stitch socket section of popper tape to lower back over raw edge, making sure the sockets line up with the ball section. Sew buttons to right back edge to correspond with buttonholes. Sew a press stud to upper neck edge at back above buttonhole.

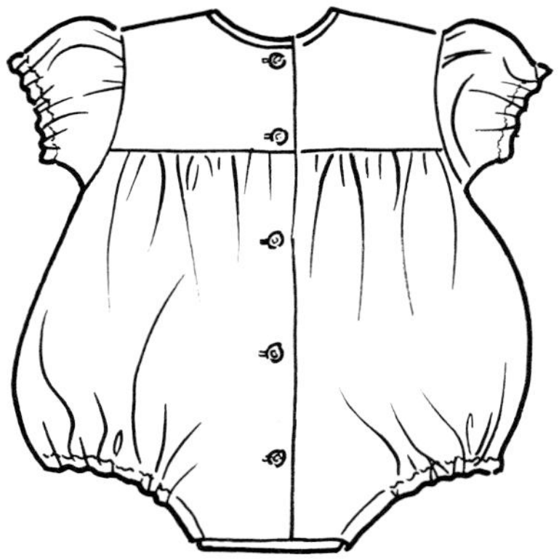

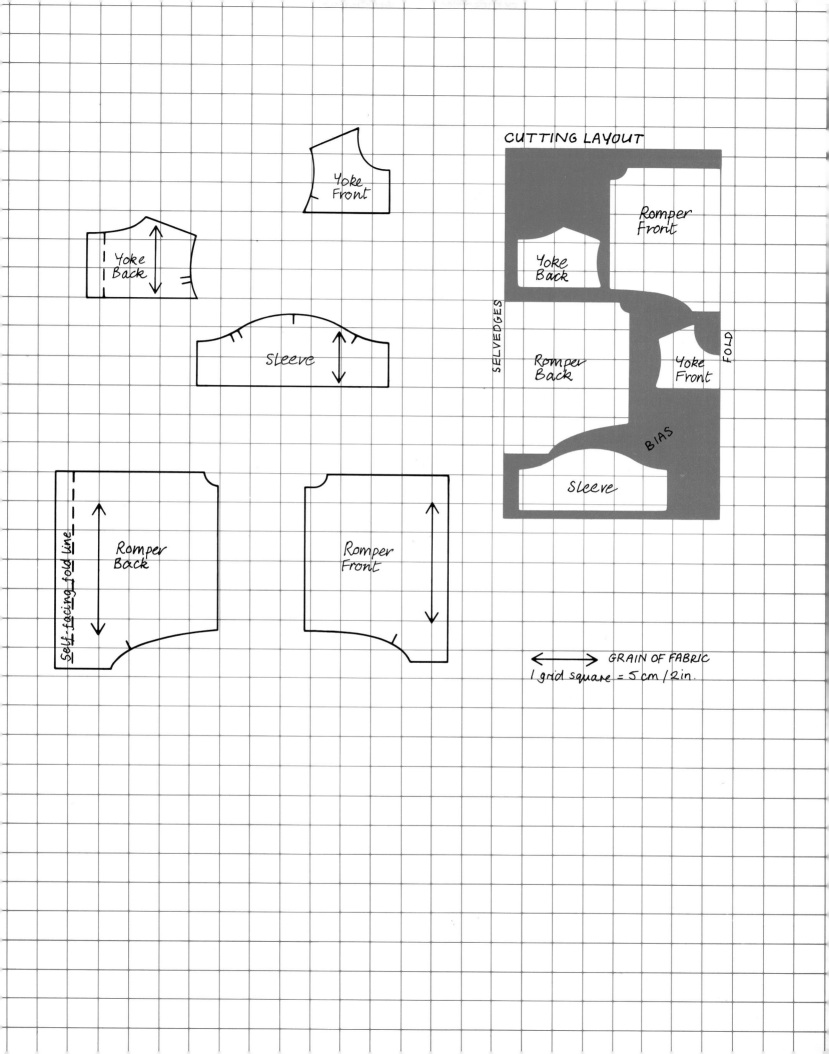

Yoke
Front

Yoke
Back

Sleeve

Self facing fold line

Romper
Back

Romper
Front

CUTTING LAYOUT

Romper
Front

Yoke
Back

SELVEDGES

Romper
Back

Yoke
Front

FOLD

BIAS

Sleeve

GRAIN OF FABRIC
1 grid square = 5 cm / 2 in.

Fairisle sweater

The fairisle sweater has been a favourite for many years. It is warm, hard wearing and will do for either a boy or a girl. This particular example is knitted in Patons Moorland Shetland double knitting, which is hand washable. The colours chosen here are autmnal shades of browns and oatmeal, but there is nothing to stop you choosing blues with a touch of red (a rather more traditional combination) or lavender and heathery shades, both with oatmeal. When knitting this pattern, take particular care not to pull the yarn too tight across the back of the work. And to follow the chart, use a rule to mark the line that you are working on.

Materials: 2(2,3) balls (50g) Patons Moorland Shetland DK in main colour (M.); 1(1,1) ball in 1st contrast; 1(1,1) ball in 2nd contrast; 1(2,2) balls in 3rd contrast and 1(1,1) ball each in 4th and 5th contrasts; pair each 3¼mm and 4mm (No. 10 and No. 8) Milward knitting needles.

Measurements: to fit 51cm (56, 61)/20in (22, 24) chest. Length 34cm (39, 42)/ 13⅜in (15⅜, 16½). Sleeve seam 21cm (24, 26)/8¼in (9½, 10¼).

Tension: 24 sts. and 26 rows to 10cm/4in square in pattern.

Abbreviations: k., knit; p., Purl; sts., stitches; cm, centimetre(s); in, inch(es); dec., decreas(e)ing; foll., following; inc., increas(e)ing; patt., pattern; rem., remain(ing); rep., repeat; sl., slip; inc.1 k., increase 1 knitwise by picking up loop between sts. and knitting into back of it.

Note: figures in brackets refer to larger sizes; where only one figure is given, this refers to all sizes.

The back
With 3¼mm/No. 10 needles and M., cast on 54(60,66) sts. Work 4cm (5, 6)/ 1½in (2, 2⅜) k.2, p.2 rib, beg. alt. rows p.2 for 1st and 3rd sizes only. *Inc. row*: rib 5(8,11), (inc.1 k., rib 3) 16 times, rib 1(4,7). 70(76,82) sts.

Change to 4mm/No. 8 needles. Reading chart from right to left on k. rows and from left to right on p. rows, cont. thus:
1st size only: *1st row*: rep. 14 sts. from C to D to end. *2nd row*: rep. 14 sts. from D to C to end.
2nd size only: *1st row*: work sts. from B to C, then rep. 14 sts. from C to D to last 3 sts., work sts. from D to E. *2nd row*: work sts. from E to D, then rep. 14 sts. from D to C to last 3 sts., work sts. from C to B.
3rd size only: *1st row*: Work sts. from A to C, then rep. 14 sts. from C to D to last 6 sts., work sts. from D to F. *2nd row*: work sts. from F to D, then rep. 14 sts. from D to C to last 6 sts., work sts. from C to A.
All sizes: cont. in this way until the 52nd row of chart has been worked. These 52 rows form the patt. Cont. in patt. until work measures 23cm (27, 29)/9in (10⅝, 11½)in, ending after p. row.
Shape armholes: cast off 3 sts. at beg. of

next 2 rows. Dec. 1 st. at both ends of next row and foll. alt. rows to 52(56,60) sts. Cont. straight until armholes measure 11cm (12, 13)/ 4⅜in (4¾, 5⅛), ending after p. row.
Shape shoulders: cast off 5 sts. at beg. of next 4 rows; 3(4,5) sts. at beg. of next 2 rows. Leave rem. 26(28,30) sts. on spare needle.

The front
Work as for back until front measures 10 rows less than back to shoulders, thus ending after p. row.
Shape neck: next row: patt. 18, turn and leave rem. sts. on spare needle. Dec. 1 st. at neck edge on next 5 rows. Work 4 rows straight, thus ending armhole edge.
Shape shoulder: cast off 5 sts. at beg. of next row and foll. alt. row. Work 1 row straight . Cast off rem. 3(4,5) sts. With right side facing, sl. centre 16(18,20) sts. on spare needle, join yarn to rem. sts. and work to match 1st side, reversing shapings.

The sleeves
With 3¼mm/No. 10 needles and M., cast on 32(36,40) sts. Work 4cm (5, 6)/ 1½in (2, 2⅜) k.2, p.2 rib. *Inc. row*: rib 2(1,7), * inc. 1 k., rib 3(3,2); rep. from * to last 3(2,7) sts., inc.1 k., rib to end. 42(48,54) sts.

Change to 4mm/No. 8 needles. Beg. with 7th(9th,11th) row of chart, cont. in patt. as for back, inc. 1 st. at both ends of 3rd(9th,11th) row and every foll. 10th row to 50(56,62) sts. Cont. straight until sleeve measures approx 21cm (24, 26)/ 8¼in (9½, 10¼), ending after same patt. row as back and front.
Shape top: cast off 3 sts. at beg. of next 2 rows. Dec. 1 st. at both ends of every row to 32(38,32) sts. Cast off 3 sts. at beg. of next 6(8,6) rows. Cast off rem. sts.

The neckband
Join right shoulder seam. With right side facing, using 3¼mm/No. 10 needles and M., pick up and k. 14 sts. down left front neck, k. centre front sts. inc. 2 sts. evenly, pick up and k. 14 sts. up right front neck, k. centre back sts. inc. 2 sts. evenly. 74(78,82) sts. Work 5cm/2in k.2, p.2 rib, beg. alt. rows p.2. Cast off loosely in rib.

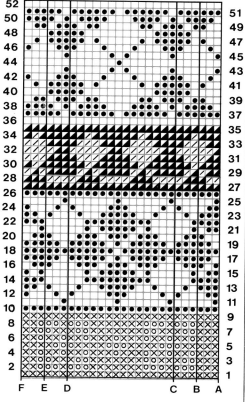

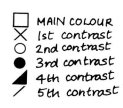

☐ MAIN COLOUR
✕ 1st contrast
○ 2nd contrast
● 3rd contrast
◣ 4th contrast
╱ 5th contrast

To make up
Press following instructions on ball band. Join left shoulder and neckband seam. Join side and sleeve seams. Sew in sleeves. Fold neckband in half to wrong side and sl. stitch.

Picture sweater

This semi-educational children's sweater was designed exclusively for us by Sally Muir and Jo Osborne, the partnership of Warm and Wonderful. They are, of course, well known for their beautiful picture sweaters, including the famous 'Black Sheep' sweater worn by Princess Diana. This sweater is made in Patons Clansman 4 ply, which is machine washable (no hotter than 40°C). A useful tip when knitting this sweater: be careful when changing colours and twist the wool on the wrong side to lock it so that you don't get holes. You can certainly use different colour combinations when knitting this sweater, but don't use a different yarn.

Materials: 3(4,4) balls (50g) Patons Clansman in main colour (M.); 1 ball in each of 3 contrasting colours (A.,B. and C.); a pair each 2¾mm and 3¼mm (No. 12 and No. 10) Milward knitting needles.

Measurements: to fit 51cm (56, 61)/20in (22, 24) chest. Length 33cm (37, 41)/13in (14½, 16). Sleeve seam 21cm (23, 27)/ 8¼in (9, 10½).

Tension: 28 sts. and 36 rows to 10cm/4in square.

Abbreviations: k., knit; p., Purl; sts., stitches; cm, centimetre(s); in, inch(es); alt., alternate; beg., beginning; cont., continue; dec., decreas(e)ing; foll., following; inc., increas(e)ing; patt., pattern; rem., remain(ing); rep., repeat; sl., slip; st.-st., stocking stitch; tog., together; inc.1 k., increase 1 by picking up loop that lies between sts. and knitting into back of it.

Note: figures in brackets refer to larger sizes; where only one figure is given, this refers to all sizes.

The back

With 2¾mm/No. 12 needles and M., cast on 68(76,84) sts. Work 4cm (5, 6)/ 1½in (2, 2⅜) k.1, p.1 rib. *Inc. row*: rib 7(11,15), (inc.1 k., rib 6) 10 times, rib 1(5,9). 78(86,94) sts.

Change to 3¼mm/No. 10 needles. Beg. k. row, work 2(10,16) rows st.-st. Reading k. rows from right to left and p. rows from left to right, twisting yarns on wrong side when changing colour to avoid a hole, work 1st to 52nd rows from chart A. Work should measure approx. 19cm (22, 25)/7½in (8⅝, 9¾).
Shape Raglan. Still working from chart, cast off 4(5,6) sts. at beg. of next 2 rows. Dec. 1 st. at both ends of next row and every foll. 4th row to 60(66,72) sts. Work 3 rows straight. Dec, 1 st. at both ends of next row and foll. 4 alt. rows. 84th row of chart has now been worked. Cont. with M. dec. at raglan on next row and foll. alt. rows as before to 32(34,36) sts., ending after p. row. Leave sts. on spare needle.

The front

Working chart B in place of 'bucket and spade', work as for back until the 84th row of chart has been worked. Cont. with M., dec. at raglan on next row and foll. alt. rows as before to 48(50,52) sts., ending after p. row. *Shape Neck. Next row*: k.2 tog., k 13, turn and leave rem. sts. on spare needle. Dec. at raglan on alt. rows as before, *at the same time* dec. 1 st. at neck edge on next row and foll. alt. rows to 3 sts. Dec. at raglan only until all sts. are worked off. With right side facing, sl. centre 18(20,22) sts. on spare needle, join yarn to rem. sts. and work to match 1st side, reversing shapings.

Sleeves

With 2¾mm/No. 12 needles and M., cast on 46(50,54) sts. Work 4cm (5, 6)/ 1½in (2, 2⅜) k.1, p.1 rib. *Inc. row*: rib 2(4,6), (inc.1 k., rib 2) 21 times, inc.1 k., rib 2(4,6). 68(72,76) sts.

Change to 3¼mm/No. 10 needles. Beg. k. row, work 4(8,18) rows st.-st. Now work in patt. from Chart C until the 58th row has been worked. Sleeve should measure approx. 21cm (23, 27)/8¼in (9, 10½).
Shape Raglan: still working from chart, cast off 4(5,6) sts. at beg. of next 2 rows. Dec 1 st. at both ends of next row and foll. alt. rows to 18(20,22) sts. Work 1 row. The 102nd row has now been worked. Cont. with M., dec. as before to 16(12,8) sts., ending after p. row. *For 1st and 2nd sizes only*: dec. 1 st at both ends of every row to 8 sts. *For all sizes*: leave rem. 8 sts. on a safety pin.

The neckband

Join both front and right back raglan seams. With right side facing, using 2¾mm/No. 12 needles and M., k. left sleeve sts., pick up and k. 14 sts. down left front neck, k. centre front sts., pick up and k. 14 sts. up right front neck, k. right sleeve and back sts. Work 5cm/2in k.1, p.1 rib. Cast off loosely in rib.

To make up

Press, following instructions on ball band. Join left raglan and neckband seam. Join side and sleeve seams. Fold neckband in half to wrong side and sl.stitch. With black yarn, embroider features on face of 'teddy bear'.

See plan overleaf.

Chart A

84 82 80 78 76 74 72 70 68 66 64 62 60 58 56 54 52 50 48 46 44 42 40 38 36 34 32 30 28 26 24 22 20 18 16 14 12 10 8 6 4 2

83 81 79 77 75 73 71 69 67 65 63 61 59 57 55 53 51 49 47 45 43 41 39 37 35 33 31 29 27 25 23 21 19 17 15 13 11 9 7 5 3 1

1
2
3

78 stitches
86 stitches
94 stitches

Dungarees

Dungarees are one of the modern classics of children's wear. They suit almost any age, from crawling onwards, and they are comfortable, durable and suitable for both boys and girls. This outfit was made up in denim, probably the favourite fabric for dungarees, but they can also look very good in stripey cotton ticking, corduroy (preferably needlecord) or heavy cotton drill. Avoid anything too harsh or stiff. Plain fabrics will do as well as printed ones, and colours can change their whole appearance: bright pink or bold electric blue are both shades that take the basic garment into the fashion arena.

Size: to fit 1½-2½ year old (3/4, 5/6). Inside leg measurement 31.5cm (37.5, 46.5)/12½in (14¾, 18¼).

Materials: 1.20m (1.40, 1.60)/1⅜yd (1⅝, 1¾) of 90cm/36in wide fabric. 6 jeans shank buttons plus fixing tool.
Pair of 25mm/1in overall buckles.
Reel of contrast buttonhole thread.
Matching thread.

Cutting out: follow cutting layout to cut out 2 fronts, 2 backs, 1 front facing and 1 pocket.

Special note: buy special jeans machine needles that are extra strong and use a special jeans foot if your machine has one: this makes sewing over bulky seams much easier. Otherwise sew slowly but steadily, never forcing the needle, and if the machine baulks at 'lumps' caused by several seam allowances meeting at the same spot, tuck a wad of folded over excess fabric under the foot behind and close up to the needle: this will help the needle over the obstacle.

Seam allowances of 15mm/⅝in are included in the pattern unless stated otherwise.

Making up
Fold back extensions along foldline, right sides inside, and stitch across upper edge. Trim seam allowances and turn extension to right side: press along foldline. Turn under remaining seam allowances along upper edge, round strap, and down to centre back. Using contrast buttonhole thread, top-stitch close to all edges, and across extension, then top stitch again 6mm/¼in from first top-stitching: press.
Right sides together, pin and stitch centre back seam: clipping curve so seam lies flat, press to one side. Top-stitch twice as before. Right sides together, pin and stitch centre front seam: clip curve so seam lies flat, press to same side as centre back seam. Top-stitch twice as before.
Turn under seam allowance on upper edge of pocket and press: top-stitch twice as before. Turn under seam allowances on remaining pocket edges, folding under corners neatly. Press, and pin to right side of front where marked. Top-stitch in place twice as before.
Pin and stitch front facing to front, right sides together, starting and stopping at +. Trim seam allowances and corners and turn to right side: press. Pin and stitch front to back at sides below + and press towards front. Top-stitch twice as before, up to +. Now top-stitch faced front twice, starting and stopping at +.
Pin and stitch front to back at inside leg seams in one movement, right sides together: press open. Turn up 15mm/⅝in hem and top-stitch twice in place. Make buttonholes at side front where marked. Attach shank buttons to upper front and side back where marked. Slot strap ends through overall buckles.

See cutting out plan overleaf.

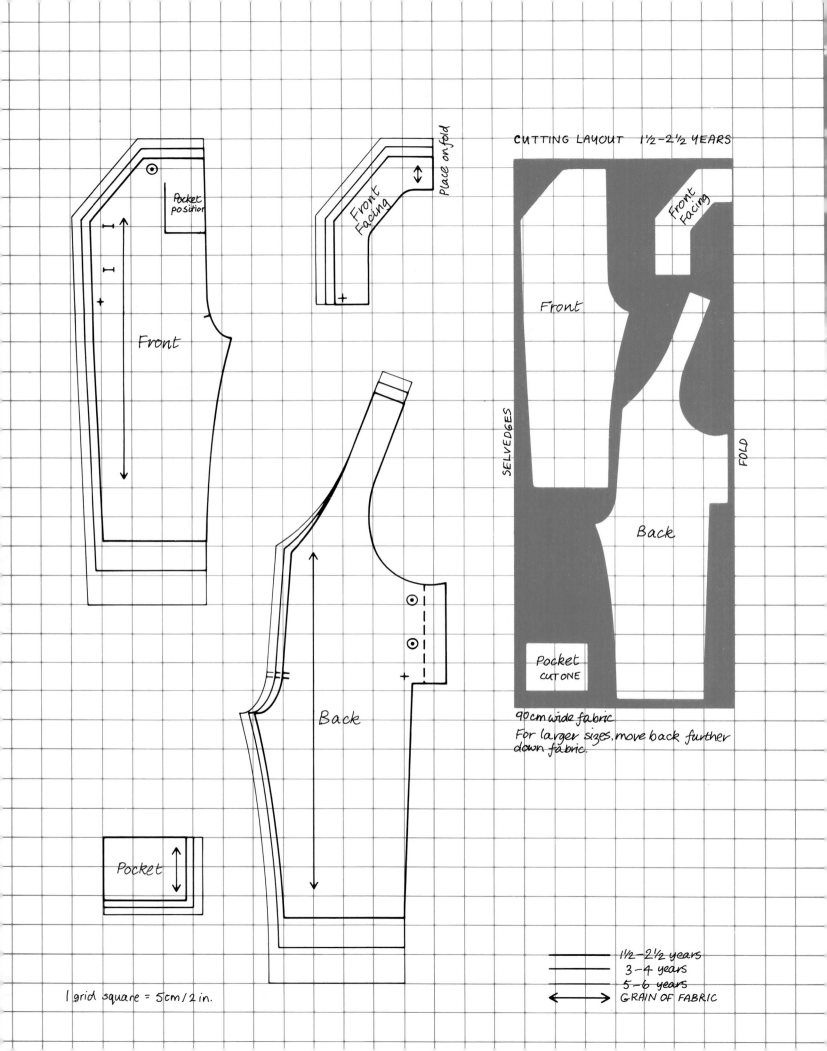

Pocket position

⊙

Front

Place on fold

Front Facing

CUTTING LAYOUT 1½–2½ YEARS

Front Facing

SELVEDGES

Front

FOLD

Back

Back

⊙
⊙

Pocket
CUT ONE

90 cm wide fabric
For larger sizes, move back further
down fabric.

Pocket

1 grid square = 5 cm/2 in.

1½–2½ years
3–4 years
5–6 years
⟷ GRAIN OF FABRIC

Girl's dress

This classic smocked-front dress has been made in a small-spotted Viyella, giving it a very traditional feel. However, it could easily be made in a wide range of fabrics, from tartan to velvet, from lightweight wool to brushed cotton or, for party wear, in self-spotted voile. For a special occasion, you could add a small detachable lace collar, or even have a pretty petticoat peeping out below the hem.

Size: to fit 1½-2½ year old (3/4, 5/6). Actual length from nape of neck 52cm (58, 67)/20½in (22¾, 26½).

Materials: 1.30m (1.70, 1.90)/1½yds (1⅞, 2⅛) of 115cm/45in wide fabric. 30cm (35, 35)/12in (14, 14) lightweight zip.
Lightweight iron-on Vilene.
Shirring elastic.
Matching thread.
Hook and eye.

Cutting out: follow cutting layout to cut out dress, cutting a strip of bias for neck binding 48mm/1⅞in wide by approximately 40cm/16in long where marked. Cut out 2 sleeve bands in Vilene.

Special note: there are two ways of machine smocking, one rather more successful than the other, but both satisfactory. *Either* wind shirring elastic by hand onto the bobbin, use ordinary thread on the top, and experiment with the tension until you get the required amount of gathering when you stitch a straight seam: *or*, and this one works best, use a zig-zag stitch on the wrong side of the fabric with ordinary thread top and bottom, sewing over but not through the shirring elastic which you guide along the seamline. Some modern machines have feet specially designed for this task. Draw up the elastic as you will afterwards.

Seam allowances of 15mm/⅝in are included in the pattern unless stated otherwise.

Making up
Dress: run two rows of machine gathering 15mm/⅝in and 10mm/⅜in from top edge of front and back skirts, starting and stopping 15mm/⅝in from the sides. On wrong side of front, for smocking lines, draw four horizontal parallel lines with tailors chalk 1cm/⅜in apart, starting 1cm/⅜in below gathering line and 3cm/1⅛in in from sides. Machine smock along these lines (see special note) and draw up elastic *gently* and evenly until front measures same as lower edge of yoke front. Secure all ends very firmly. Now draw up gathering threads evenly at upper edge of skirt front and pin and sew to yoke front, right

sides together. Stitch again 6mm/¼in inside first stitching and trim close to this stitching. Over-sew these edges together with a zig-zag or special overcasting stitch if available. Draw up gathering threads evenly at upper edge of skirt backs and pin and sew to yoke backs, right sides together. Stitch again 6mm/¼in inside first stitching and trim close to this stitching. Oversew as for front.

Pin and stitch yoke front to yoke backs at shoulder seams, right sides together, and press seams open. Pin and stitch centre back seam up to zip notch, right sides together, and press seam open and remaining seam allowances to wrong side. Insert zip so that zip pull lies 15mm/⅝in below neck edge.

Neckband: stay-stitch neck edge by machining 1cm/⅜in from raw edge, using small stitches. Press under 12mm/½in on each long edge of neck binding and allow to cool completely. Open out one fold and pin to right side of neck edge, extending binding 1cm/⅜in beyond centre back opening and stretching binding slightly as you go. Stitch along fold line, trim seam allowances to 6mm/¼in and press towards binding. Tucking under ends at centre back, slip-stitch remaining edge of bias binding over first stitching: press.

Sleeves: fuse Vilene to wrong side of sleeve bands and press under 15mm/⅝in on each long edge: allow to cool completely. Run two rows of machine gathering 15mm/⅝in and 10mm/⅜in from lower edge of sleeve, and round sleevehead inbetween notches. Pull up gathers at lower edge of sleeve until it measures the same as the sleeve band. Open out one fold of sleeve band and pin to lower edge of sleeve, right sides together, distributing gathers evenly. Stitch along fold line: trim seam allowance to 6mm/¼in and press towards sleeve band. Now pin sleevehead to armhole, right sides together, matching notches, shoulder notches and sides and pulling up gathers evenly. Stitch and stitch again 6mm/¼in inside first stitching: trim seam allowances close to this stitching. Overcast as before

and press seam towards sleeve.

Sides: pin and stitch side and sleeve seams in one, right sides together: press open. Pin remaining edge of sleeve band to wrong side over first stitching: slip-stitch in place: press.

Hem: turn up 6cm/2¼in hem and tack in place. Slip-stitch invisibly and press. Sew hook and eye to neck band ends above zip pull.

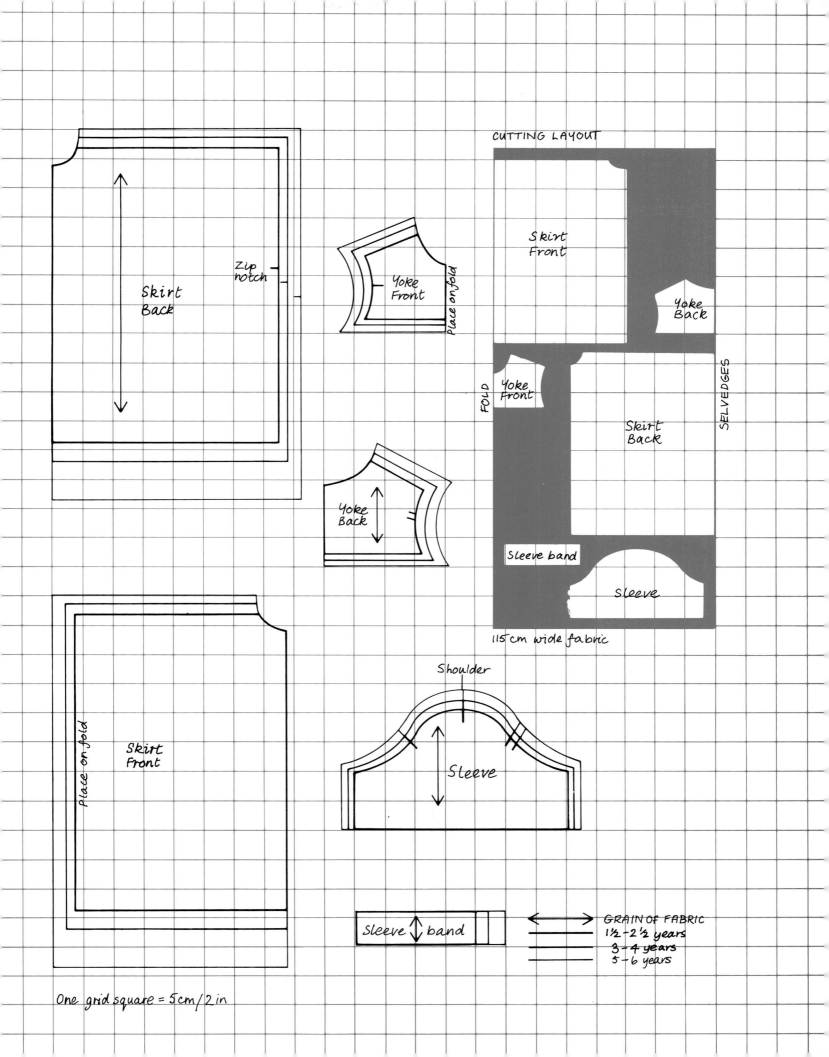

Skirt Back

Zip notch

Yoke Front

Place on fold

CUTTING LAYOUT

Skirt Front

Yoke Back

FOLD

Yoke Front

SELVEDGES

Skirt Back

Yoke Back

Sleeve band

Sleeve

115 cm wide fabric

Place on fold

Skirt Front

Shoulder

Sleeve

Sleeve band

GRAIN OF FABRIC
1½ - 2½ years
3 - 4 years
5 - 6 years

One grid square = 5cm / 2 in

Kilts

The fabric chosen for this kilt was an appropriate one – a Viyella tartan called 'Queen Victoria'. However, this pattern would work for a wide range of other tartans or checks. But do remember to keep the pattern small. For small children, you don't need a great deal of fabric, and a bold pattern is lost. Remember too that the pleats should match the pattern recurrence, so choose one that doesn't lead you into outsize pleats. Kilts always look good worn with sweaters, especially arans or fairisles, as well as with simple blouses. Colourful tights or socks are best, with simple pumps or barshoes for footwear.

Size: to fit up to 4 years. For larger sizes, adjust length accordingly and add width by inserting one or more extra pleats in main piece the same width as standard pleats, i.e. 4cm/1½in. For smaller sizes, adjust length accordingly and eliminate one pleat or more. Remember to adjust the waistband by the same amount.

Materials: 80cm/⅞yd of 115cm/45in wide fabric.
1 leather kilt buckle fastening.
1 kilt pin.
1 15mm/½in flat button.
1 press stud.
Medium Vilene Fold-a-Band for waistband.
Matching thread.

Cutting out: follow graph pattern to make a paper pattern using dressmakers' 5cm/2in squared pattern paper. Follow cutting layout and cut out. Cut a piece of Vilene Fold-a-Band the same length as the waistband.

Special note: this pattern has been specially designed for a 10cm/4in repeat check. For any other width pattern repeat, you will have to replan the graph pattern, so that each pleat is the same width as the pattern repeat, whilst allowing for the fact that the distance between each pleat will be different. The unpleated parts of the pattern can be left untouched. *This is not recommended for any but the experienced.*

Seam allowances of 15mm/⅝in are included in the pattern.

Making up
Stitch both front darts and press towards sides. Pin and stitch main piece to right front at side seam, right sides facing, and press open. Turn up the hem – 4cm/1½in is allowed for but adjust if necessary. Catch-stitch in place and press.

Fold the skirt along each solid pleat line on the right side: tack and press. Bring fold up to dotted pleat line and tack in place. Top stitch close to fold from upper edge to 12cm/4¾in below upper edge: press.

Turn under self-facings at each front edge and press: tack upper edges together along seamline. Slip-stitch lower edges together and up to top edge of hem.

Fuse Vilene to wrong side of waistband. Pin and stitch waistband to upper edge of kilt, right sides facing, so that ends extend 15mm/⅝in at front edges, matching right side seam to notch and left side dart to notch. Trim seam allowances and press towards waistband. Fold waistband in half, right side inside, and stitch across ends. Trim seam allowances and turn to right side. Fold waistband along upper edge and turn under remaining seam allowances: slip-stitch in place over first stitching: press. Top-stitch all round waistband close to edges.

Lap right front over left up to left front dart, and stitch kilt buckle fastening to waistband. Sew a press stud to waistband and underneath kilt buckle to stop it sagging. Make a buttonhole in left front waistband at end: sew button to correspond on wrong side of right front waistband. Pin on kilt pin. Remove all tackings.

See cutting out plan overleaf.

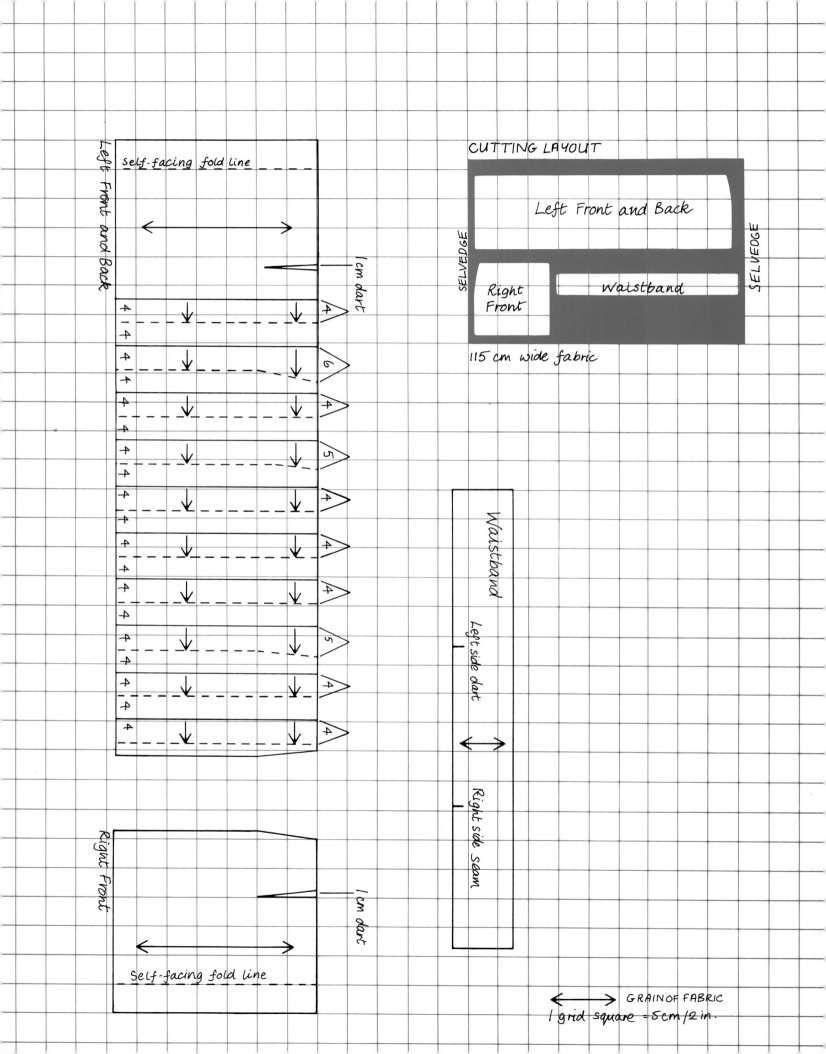

Left Front and Back

Self-facing fold line

1 cm dart

4
4 4
4 6
4 4
4 5
4 4
4 4
4 4
4 5
4 4
4

Right Front

1 cm dart

Self-facing fold line

CUTTING LAYOUT

Left Front and Back

SELVEDGE

Right
Front
Waistband

SELVEDGE

115 cm wide fabric

Waistband

Left side dart

Right side seam

GRAIN OF FABRIC

1 grid square = 5 cm/2 in.

Sailor suits

Sailor suits can look adorable on both boys and girls. They seem to suit more or less any child. Among older children, girls probably have more chances to wear suits like this than boys, but the pattern here would make a super page-boy outfit for a wedding. Because they are so classic in style, stick to the classic colours of blue and white. A white sailor suit trimmed in blue can look as attractive as a blue sailor suit trimmed in white. We chose Viyella for the two suits shown here because it is hard wearing, and you can therefore team up the girl's skirt and the boy's trousers with sweaters or other shirts, giving the suit more mileage. Heavy, crisp cotton would also be ideal for summer, and a wool blend or very fine baby cord for winter.

Size: to fit 1½-2½ year old (3/4, 5/6). Shirt length 31cm/12¼in. Trouser length 26cm (28, 32)/10¼in (11, 12½). Skirt length 23cm (25, 28)/9in (9¾, 11).

Materials: 90cm (1m, 1.10m)/1yd (1⅛, 1¼) of 140 or 150cm/56 or 60in wide fabric for trouser suit.
60cm/¾yd of 115cm/45in wide contrast fabric for shirt.
40cm/16in of lightweight Vilene Supershape for shirt.
40cm/16in of 3cm/1in medium Vilene Fold-a-Band for trousers.
1.80m/2yds of 6mm/¼in flat braid for shirt.
12cm (15, 15)/5in (6, 6) trouser zip.
30cm/12in of 25mm/1in elastic for trousers.
60cm/¾yd of 20mm/¾in elastic for skirt.
1 15mm/⅝in button for trousers.
Matching and contrast threads.

Cutting out: Follow graph pattern to make a paper pattern using dressmakers' 5cm/2in squared pattern paper. Follow cutting layout for appropriate garment. From Vilene cut two front waistbands for trousers using Fold-a-Band, 1 collar, 1 front neck facing and 1 back neck facing from Supershape for shirt.

Special note: Always pre-wash braid before applying to garment, using the same temperature wash you intend to use for the finished garment. This will ensure any shrinking occurs *before* the braid is permanently applied, and will also enable any loose dye to be safely washed out in advance.

Seam allowances of 15mm/⅝in are included in the pattern unless stated otherwise.

Making up
Trousers: pin and stitch one back to one front at side and inside leg seams right sides facing: press open. Repeat for other leg. Turn one leg to right side and slot inside other leg right sides are facing, matching centre fronts, centre backs and inside leg seams. Pin and stitch crutch seam from centre back to lower edge of zip opening: stitch again 6mm/¼in inside first stitching round curved part only, trim close to second

stitching, clipping seam allowances above and below: overcast seam allowances together, press remaining centre back seam open. Press left centre front seam allowance to wrong side along centre front foldline. Press right centre front seam allowance to wrong side along right front foldline. Lay zip right side up under centre front opening, having zip pull 2cm/¾in below upper raw edge, and pin right front foldline close up to zip teeth: stitch close to fold using zipper foot on machine. Lap left front over right, matching centre fronts (left overlaps right by 1cm/⅜in) and pin to remaining left side of zip. Stitch through all thicknesses along stitching line using zipper foot. Strengthen lower end of zip opening with 1cm/⅜in of close zig-zag stitching.

Fuse Vilene Fold-a-Band to wrong side of front waistbands following instructions on packet. Pin and stitch to back waistband at sides, right sides facing, up to halfway point only: press seams open and remaining seam allowances to wrong side along seamline. Pin waistband to upper edge of trousers, right sides facing, matching sides seams, centre fronts and centre backs: stitch. Trim seam allowances to 6mm/¼in and press towards waistband. Fold waistband in half, right side inside, and stitch across ends: trim seam allowances and turn to right side. Turn under remaining front waistband seam allowances and pin over first stitching: slip-stitch in place, slip-stitching left front overlap seam allowances together: press. Pin remaining back waistband seam allowance over first stitching so that seam allowance extends below waistband: stitch from right side along first stitching line. Cut elastic

to fit and slot through casing thus formed, through openings in waistband side seams so that ends extend 1cm/⅜in over each side seam. Stitch firmly in place along side seam stitching: tuck elastic ends into front waistbands and slip-stitch up openings. Turn up 3.5cm/1⅜in hemsor to suit and catch stitch invisibly in place.

Skirt: pin and stitch the four skirt sections together at side seams, right sides facing, leaving upper 3cm/1¼in on one seam open: press open. Turn upper edge to wrong side 3cm/1¼in from edge and press. Stitch 2.5cm/1in from fold. (Gap in one seam will become opening for elastic). Cut elastic to fit waist plus 2cm/¾in: slot through casing, overlap ends 1cm/⅜in each and stitch securely together down middle. Tuck ends inside casing and slip-stitch up opening. Turn up 3.5cm/1⅜in hem or to suit and catch-stitch invisibly in place: press.

Shirt: fold ties in half lengthwise, right sides inside, and stitch along one short end and long edge. Trim seam allowances and corners and turn to right side: press. Pin unfinished end to front shoulder seam on right side, 3cm/1¼in in from neck edge, having raw edges even: tack in place along seamline. Pin and stitch front to back at shoulders, right sides facing: press open, pressing tie end towards back.

Fuse Vilene to wrong side of one collar: pin and stitch both collars together, right sides inside, round outer edges only. Trim seam allowances and corners, turn to right side and press. Tack neck edges together along seamline. Tack braid to uninterfaced side of collar 12mm/½in in from outer edges, making neat corners at back, and stitch in place close to each edge of braid: press. Fuse Vilene to wrong side of front and back neck facings: pin and stitch together at shoulders, right sides facing: press open, overcast outer edge. Reinforce lower point of V by stitching along seamline either side of V with small stitches: clip to stitching at V. Pin wrong side of collar to right side of shirt neck edge, matching notches and shoulders: tack along seamline. Pin right side of neck facings to right side of collar, matching notches and shoulder seams, pulling points of collar through slash in facing: stitch, trim seam allowances and clip curves. Press seam allowances towards facing and understitch facing close to seam through all thicknesses to prevent facing rolling out. Turn and press facing to wrong side, and catch-stitch to shoulder seam allowances.

Tack braid to right side of sleeve 4.7cm/1⅞in above lower edge, and stitch in place close to each edge: press. Run two rows of gathering stitching between notches on sleevehead, 15mm/⅝in and 10mm/⅜in from raw edge. Pin sleevehead to armhole, right sides facing, matching sides, notches and shoulders, and drawing up gathers to distribute fullness evenly: stitch, stitch again 6mm/¼in inside first stitching and trim seam allowances close to second stitching. Overcast and press seam allowances towards sleeve. Pin and stitch front to back at side and sleeve seams in one continuous movement: press open. Turn up 3.5cm/1⅜in sleeve hem to inside and press: catch stitch in place. Turn up lower hem 3.5cm/1⅜in to inside and press: catch stitch in place.

CUTTING LAYOUT FOR TROUSER SUIT

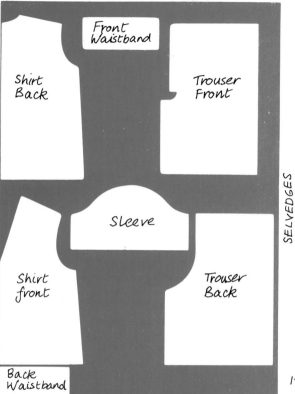

Front Waistband

Shirt Back

Trouser Front

FOLD

Sleeve

Shirt front

Trouser Back

SELVEDGES

Back Waistband

140/150 cm wide fabric

CUTTING LAYOUT FOR SKIRT SUIT

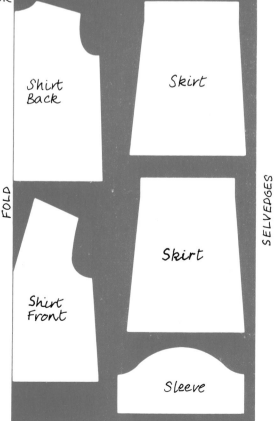

Shirt Back

Skirt

FOLD

Skirt

Shirt Front

SELVEDGES

Sleeve

115 cm wide fabric

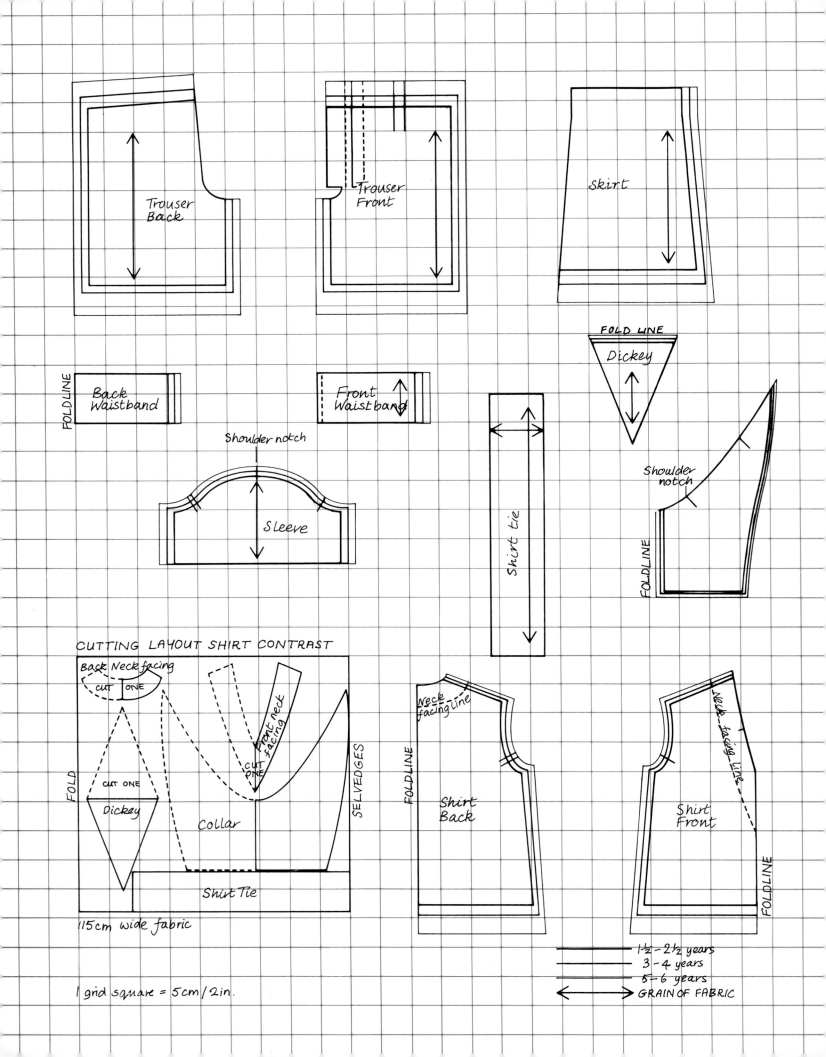

Trouser Back

Trouser Front

Skirt

FOLDLINE
Back Waistband

Front Waistband

FOLD LINE
Dickey

Shoulder notch

Sleeve

Shirt tie

Shoulder notch

FOLDLINE

CUTTING LAYOUT SHIRT CONTRAST

Back Neck facing
CUT ONE

Front neck facing
CUT ONE

FOLD

CUT ONE
Dickey

Collar

Shirt Tie

SELVEDGES

115cm wide fabric

Neck facing line

FOLDLINE

Shirt Back

Neck facing line

Shirt Front

FOLDLINE

1 grid square = 5cm/2in.

1½ – 2½ years
3 – 4 years
5 – 6 years
GRAIN OF FABRIC

Christening robe

A traditional hand-made Christening robe could well end up by being a family heirloom. Choose a fabric that is suitable for a young baby to wear, but at the same time a bit more luxurious than usual. Ours is made in a self-embroidered silk, but broderie anglaise, lace (providing it has an underdress), a polyester crêpe de chine, or a self-patterned voile would all be suitable. Because of the length of this garment, you do need a fabric that hangs well and doesn't crease too easily. The colour needs to be soft and light, white or cream being the most popular and traditional. Don't add too many extra details as they can look very fussy on such a small person.

Size: to fit up to a six month old baby.

Materials: 2.20m/2½yds of 90cm/36in wide fabric.
6.50m/7⅛yds of 6mm/¼in satin ribbon.
40cm/16in of 5mm/³⁄₁₆in elastic.
8 6mm/¼in buttons.
1 press stud.
Shirring elastic.
Matching thread.

Cutting out: follow the graph pattern to make a paper pattern using dressmakers' 5cm/2in squared pattern paper. Follow cutting layout to cut out robe. Cut a strip of bias fabric for neck binding 25mm/1in wide by approximately 30cm/12in long. Cut a straight strip of fabric for neck ruffle 42 x 5.5cm/16½ x 2⅛in: for front yoke ruffle, one strip 42 x 7cm/16½ x 2¾in: for back yoke ruffle, two strips 25 x 7cm/10 x 2¾in.

Special note: the most important thing when sewing fine silks is to have a very sharp, fine needle in the machine. The slightest burr will cause threads to snag so check your needle often. It is not necessary to use silk thread, although purists will want to. One of the finer all-purpose threads such as Gutermann or Mölnlycke will give perfect results as well as added strength to the seams. *Never* steam press or use a damp cloth with silk as it can leave watermarks: experiment with a scrap first and try a two dot setting. Use fine lace pins and try to pin only within seam allowances as pin holes can show up on silk even after pressing.

Seam allowances of 15mm/⅝in are included in the pattern, except at neck edge, where it is 6mm/¼in.

Making up: pin and sew one yoke front to two yoke backs at shoulders, right sides together: press open. Fold front yoke ruffle in half lengthwise, right side inside, and stitch across ends: trim seam allowances and turn to right side. Tack raw edges together and press. Do the same with both back yoke ruffles. Run two rows of gathering stitches 15mm/⅝in and 10mm/⅜in from raw edges of front and back ruffles. Having raw edges

even, pin front ruffle to right side of lower edge of front yoke, starting and stopping 15mm/⅝in from each side edge of yoke, pulling up gathering to fit and distributing gathers evenly: stitch, stitch again 6mm/¼in inside first stitching. Do the same with back yoke and ruffles.

Run two rows of gathering stitches at upper edge of front and back skirts, 15mm/⅝in and 10mm/⅜in from raw edges, starting and stopping 15mm/⅝in from each side for front, and for backs, at self-facing foldline and 15mm/⅝in from side. Pin front skirt to lower edge of front yoke, right sides together, matching sides, centre fronts and raw edges: pull up gathers to fit, distributing evenly, and stitch. Stitch again 6mm/¼in inside first stitching: trim close to second stitching, remove all gathering threads, and press towards yoke. Do the same with back skirts and back yokes, matching self-facing foldline to yoke centre back seamline, stopping stitching at that point. Fold skirt self-facing to wrong side and stitch down along yoke seamline. Press remaining self-facing to wrong side along its entire length.

Fold armhole ruffles in half lengthwise, wrong side inside, and tack together along raw edges. Run two rows of gathering stitches 15mm/⅝in and 10mm/⅜in from raw edges. Pin ruffle to right side of armhole edge of yoke, matching shoulders and raw edges, ending at side seams. Pull up gathers to fit, distributing them evenly, and stitch. Remove gathering thread.

Run two rows of gathering stitches 15mm/⅝in and 10mm/⅜in from raw edge of sleeveheads inbetween notches. Pin sleevehead to armhole edge of yoke, right sides facing (thus sandwiching armhole ruffle in between), matching notches, shoulders and side seams. Pull up gathers to fit, distributing them evenly, and stitch: stitch again 6mm/¼in inside first stitching and trim seam allowances close to second stitching. Press seam allowances towards yoke. For yoke lining, pin and sew remaining yoke front to remaining yoke backs at shoulders, right sides together, and press open. Press under 15mm/⅝in along lower and armhole edges, and trim to 6mm/¼in. Pin yoke lining to yoke at

centre backs, right sides together, and stitch: turn to right side and press. Pin lower and armhole edges of yoke lining to wrong side of yoke and slip-stitch in place over first stitching. Tack neck edges together. Fold neck ruffle in half lengthwise, right side inside, and stitch across ends: trim seam allowances and turn to right side. Tack raw edges together and press. Run a row of gathering stitches 6mm/¼in from raw edges. Pin ruffle to neck edge, matching raw edges and placing ends at centre back. Draw up gathers to fit, distributing them evenly. Stitch in place and remove gathering stitches. Press both long edges of bias neck binding 5mm/³⁄₁₆in to wrong side and allow to cool completely. Use this to bind neck edge, turning under ends neatly at centre back.

Turn up 3.5cm/1⅜in hem on each sleeve and press. Stitch 2cm/¾in and 2.8cm/1⅛in from fold to form casing for elastic. Cut two pieces of elastic approximately 19cm/7½in long and slot through each casing, so that ends finish at side edges. Stitch in place securely across ends.

Pin and stitch sides seams together, right sides inside, continuing stitching along sleeve seam: press open.

Turn up 15mm/⅝in hem on robe and top-stitch in place 10mm/⅜in from fold. Turn under back self facing and slip-stitch lower edges together.

Make buttonholes in left back where marked and sew buttons to right back to correspond. Sew press stud to upper edge of opening.

To make drapes at hem, on wrong side, zig-zag either side of stitching line over a piece of shirring elastic, starting at top edge and turning round at lower edge to make a loop of elastic. Pull up shirring elastic gently but completely, and secure ends firmly. Cut eight lengths of ribbon x 80cm/⅞yd, mark centre with a pin, and stitch to right side of robe at top of each drape line and to bow positions on yoke. Tie ribbon in bows and trim ends diagonally.

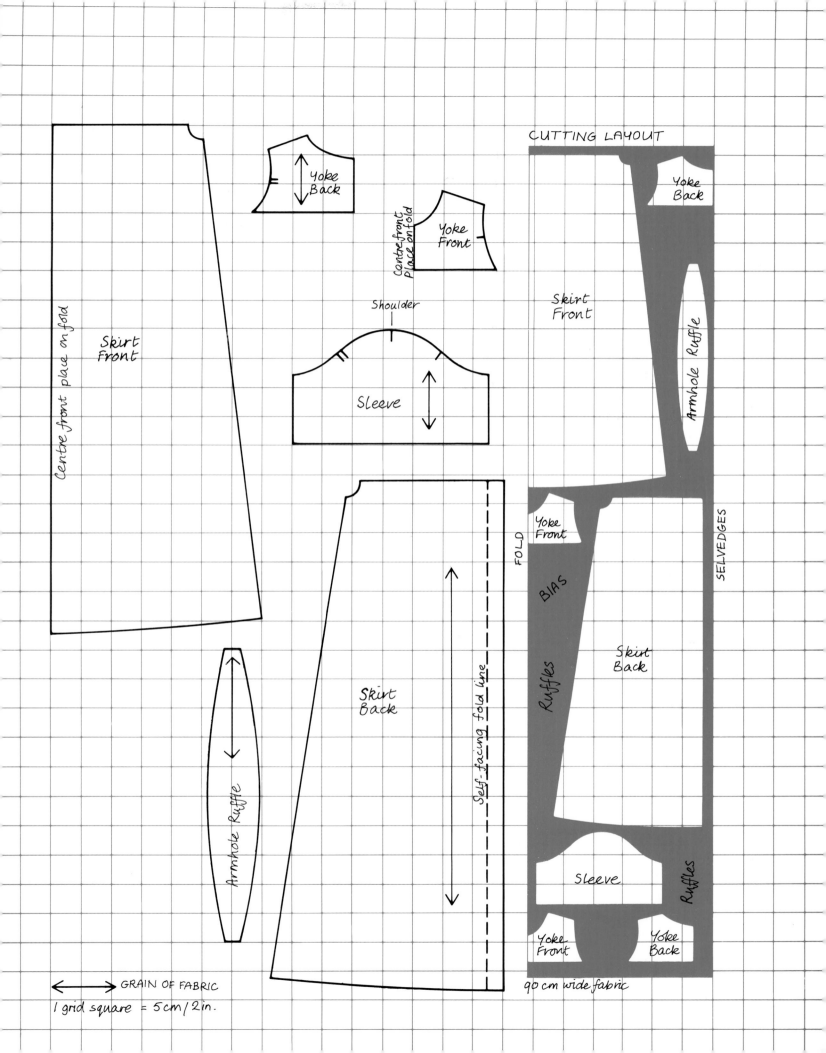

Centre front place on fold

Skirt Front

Yoke Back

Centre front place on fold

Yoke Front

Shoulder

Sleeve

FOLD

Self-facing fold line

Skirt Back

Armhole Ruffle

GRAIN OF FABRIC

1 grid square = 5cm / 2in.

CUTTING LAYOUT

Skirt Front

Yoke Back

Armhole Ruffle

Yoke Front

BIAS

Ruffles

Skirt Back

SELVEDGES

Sleeve

Ruffle

Yoke Front

Yoke Back

90 cm wide fabric

Day dress

This button-front shirt dress is in a style that can be worn either casually (neck undone, sleeves rolled back), or more formally. It is also a good dress for just after the birth of the baby, because it has a button front, and you can easily breast feed while wearing it. Choose fabrics that you know you will be comfortable in – pay attention to the time of year. We made this dress in 100% pure wool checked Viyella (please note that this must be dry cleaned, unlike other Viyella fabrics, which are hand washable), and trimmed it with a red needlecord collar, but other fabrics, including wool crêpe, brushed cotton, a wool blend, or even a good weight jersey, would all do equally well.

Size: to fit 12-16 (normal size) *very* loosely: for larger or smaller sizes, add or subtract width along a vertical line from mid-shoulder to hem, front and back equally: adjust hem and sleeve lengths appropriately.

Materials: 2.40m/2⅝yds of 150cm/60in wide fabric.
30cm/⅜yd of baby cord for collar.
Lightweight Supershape Iron-On Vilene.
7 15mm/⅝in buttons.
1m/1⅛yds of 6mm/¼in velvet ribbon to match collar.
Matching threads.

Cutting out: follow graph pattern to make a paper pattern using dressmakers' 5cm/2in squared pattern paper. Follow cutting layouts to cut out dress in main fabric and collars in contrast fabric, having pile running in the same direction smoothing from points to neck edge. Cut out two collars in Vilene (see special note). Cut two strips of Vilene 4 x 45cm/1½ x 17¾in for front extensions.

Special note: sewing with checks needs a clear head so think before you cut. Decide which part of the check you want to centre the garment on, and align centre front seam line (*not* cutting line) along this line. Make sure front and back hems finish at the same point in the check horizontally, and align centre back fold along same line of check as centre front seam line. To be sure of matching checks exactly, cut each piece separately, using first piece as pattern for second piece, remembering to turn it over so you get one left and one right piece. Pin seams at right angles check by check to make sure all checks match before machining – tack first if you want to

be absolutely sure. It takes some time to do it right, but it makes all the difference in the end. You will note both sides of the collar are lightly interfaced: this is not normal but it is to allow you to turn up the collar and wear it looking as crisp on the one side as the other.

Seam allowances of 15mm/⅝in are included in the pattern.

Making up
Fuse Vilene strips to wrong sides of extensions from foldline to raw edges. Pin and stitch centre front seam, right sides facing, up to 15mm/⅝in above lower edge of extensions: press open. Clip seam allowances up to stitching at top of seam. Press left extension to wrong side along foldline: tack lower adges and neck edges together. Fold right extension to right side along foldline and stitch lower edge from foldline to centre front seamline: trim seam allowances, clip to stitching at centre front and turn to right side. Press along foldline and stitch down extension on right side. Tack neck edges together.
  Pin and stitch front to back at shoulders, right sides facing: press open. Stay-stitch neck edge by stitching 3mm/⅛in inside seamline using small stitches.
  Make collar by fusing Vilene to wrong side of both collars. Turn under seam allowance on neck edge of one collar: press and trim to 6mm/¼in. Pin and stitch both collars together, right sides inside, along all edges but neck edge. Trim seam allowances and corners, clip seam allowances to dots and along curves where necessary and turn to right side: press. Pin and stitch unfinished neck edge of one collar to neck edge of dress, right sides facing,

matching fronts, centre backs and shoulders, clipping neck edge of dress up to but not through stay-stitching where necessary to lie flat. Trim seam allowances and press towards collar. Slip-stitch remaining neck edge of collar over first stitching. Top-stitch collar close to all edges. Pin and stitch side and sleeve seams in one continuous movement, right sides inside. Reinforce underarms by stitching again over first stitching: press seams open.
  Turn up 3cm/1¼in sleeve hems, press and slip-stitch in place.
  Turn up 15mm/⅝in hem or to suit at lower edge of dress, press and slip-stitch in place.
  Make horizontal buttonholes at right front extension, 10mm/⅜in from edge, with one in collar and others at 7cm/2¾in intervals starting 2cm/¾in below collar. Sew on buttons to left extension to correspond. Mark centre of ribbon with a pin and catch stitch to centre back just below collar. Tie in a bow at centre front.

See cutting out plan overleaf.

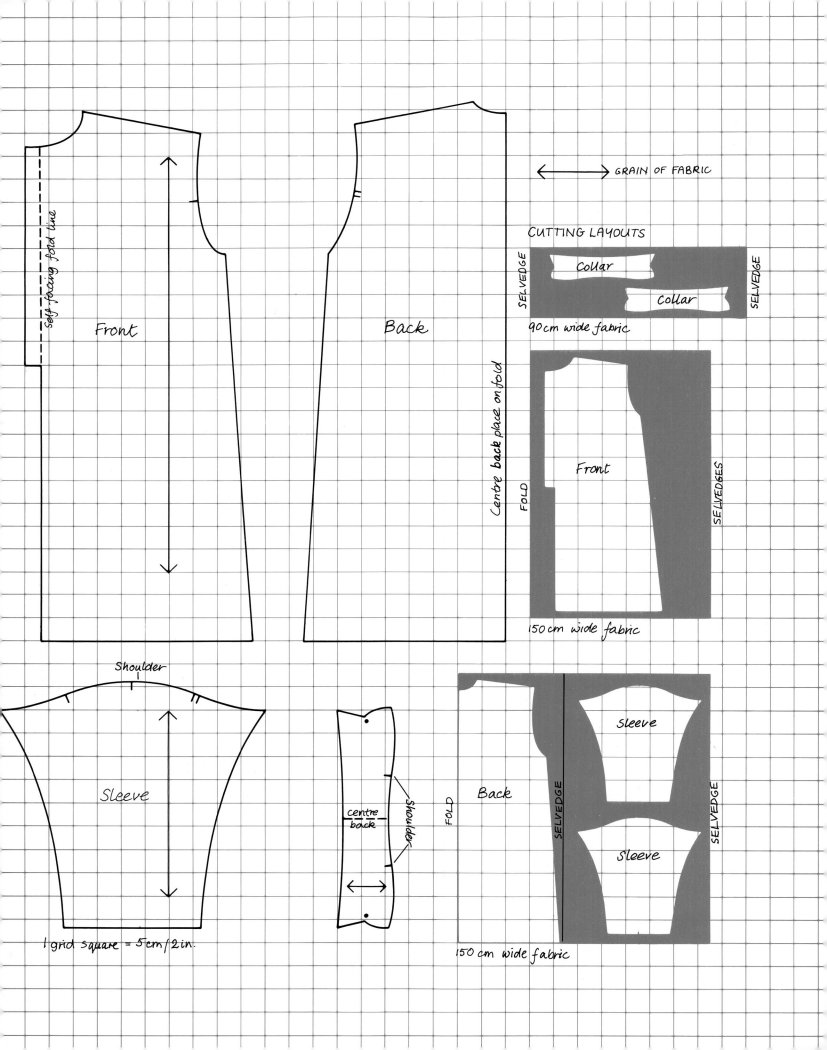

Front

self facing fold line

Back

Centre back place on fold

GRAIN OF FABRIC

CUTTING LAYOUTS

SELVEDGE

Collar

Collar

SELVEDGE

90 cm wide fabric

FOLD

Front

SELVEDGES

150 cm wide fabric

Shoulder

Sleeve

centre back

Shoulder

Sleeve

Back

FOLD

SELVEDGE

SELVEDGE

Sleeve

150 cm wide fabric

1 grid square = 5 cm/2 in.

Dungarees

This easy and comfortable outfit is great for everyday wear, providing that you are in reasonably good shape. They can, however, if you are not careful, make you look rather big and be a bit unflattering. Never wear them when they are so tight that they are pulling over the tummy. They are ideal for summer made in heavy cotton, such as a cotton drill, or, like ours, in cotton ticking. For winter, choose needlecord or denim, but do make sure that the fabric you choose is not so stiff as to make the dungarees uncomfortable – with heavier fabrics, it sometimes pays to wash them before sewing. Dungarees go well with shirts, sweaters or t-shirts, but don't overload yourself.

Size: to fit size 8-10, 12-14, 16-18 (normal sizes).

Materials: 2.60m/2⅞yds of 90cm/36in wide fabric.
40cm/16in of 2cm/¾in wide elastic.
Matching thread.

Cutting out: follow the graph pattern to make a paper pattern using dressmakers' 5cm/2in squared pattern paper. Follow cutting layout for sizes 8-10 and 12-14. For size 16-18, cut out bib first on folded fabric. Cut remaining fabric in half widthwise so you have two pieces 115cm x 90cm/45in x 36in and lay one half on top of the other, right sides facing. Lay back pattern piece to one side (left), reverse front and lay next to back (right). Fit in straps and ties alongside.

Seam allowances of 15mm/⅝in are included in the pattern.

Making up
Make 22mm/⅞in vertical buttonholes in fronts where marked, with top of buttonhole exactly 37mm/1⅜in below upper raw edge. (If liked reinforce wrong side with a square of Iron-On Vilene beforehand.)

Pin and stitch one front to one back at side and inside leg seams, right sides facing: press open. Repeat with other leg. Turn leg to right side and slot inside other leg, matching centre fronts, centre backs and inside leg seams. Pin and stitch crutch seam, right sides facing, stitch again 6mm/¼in inside first stitching and trim seam allowances close to second stitching. Overcast edges together and press seam to one side except under crutch. Pin and stitch both bib pieces together, right sides facing, leaving lower edge open. Trim seam allowances, clip curves, and turn to right side: press. Top-stitch close to finished edges and again 1cm/⅜in from edge: tack lower edges together. Make two horizontal buttonholes 22cm/⅞in long where marked. Pin bib to front of pants in between front buttonholes, right sides facing, and tack in place 6mm/¼in from edge. Stitch in place 35mm/1¼in from edge.

Make straps by folding in half lengthwise, right sides inside, and stitching along straight end and long edge. Trim seam allowances and corners and turn to right side: press and top-stitch close to all finished edges. Pin unfinished slanted ends to right side of back of pants where marked, so they 'lean' towards centre back, and tack in place 6mm/¼in from edge. Stitch in place 35mm/1¼in from edge.

Press under remaining top edge of pants by 35mm/1¼in and top-stitch 25mm/1in from fold.

Make tie ends by folding ties in half lengthwise, right sides inside, and stitching along one short and the long edge. Trim seam allowances and corners and turn to right side: press and top-stitch close to all finished edges. Overlap unfinished ends and elastic ends by 1cm/⅜in and stitch securely. Slot tie through buttonholes into upper casing so that ties extend through buttonholes.

Turn up 15mm/⅝in hem and press: top-stitch in place 1cm/⅜in from fold.

Slot strap ends through buttonholes in bib and knot.

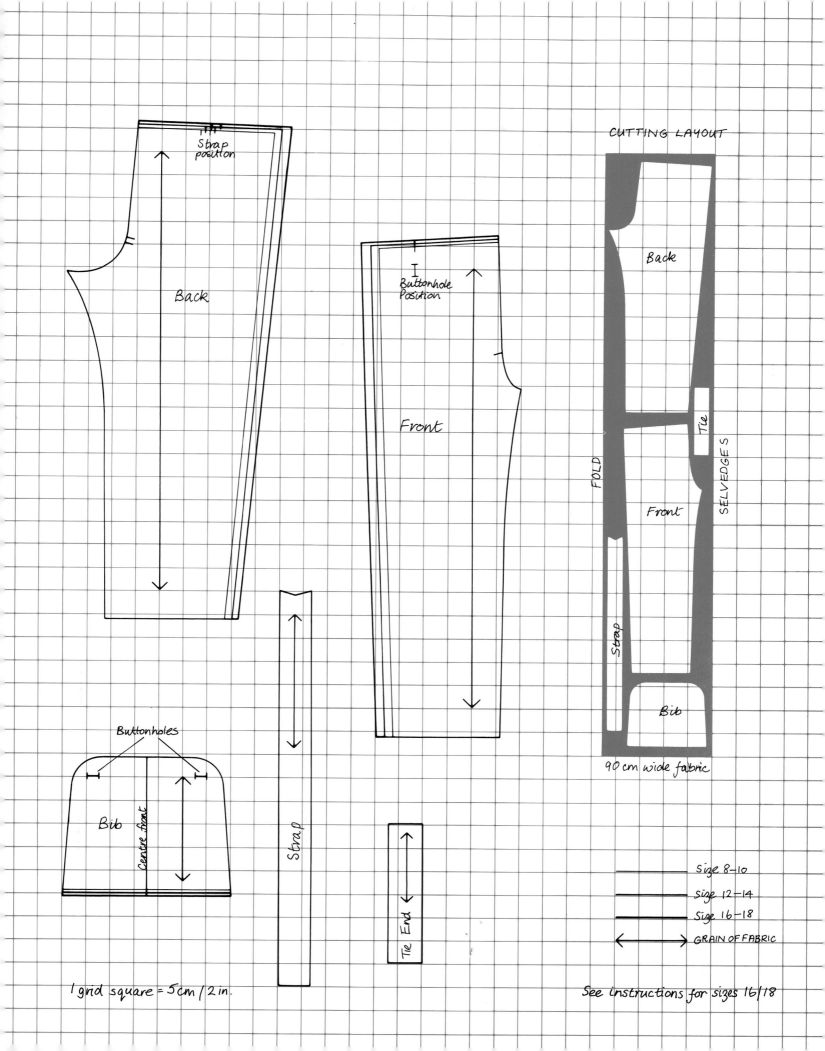

Strap position

Back

Buttonhole Position

Front

Buttonholes

Bib

Centre front

Strap

Tie End

CUTTING LAYOUT

Back

Tie

FOLD

SELVEDGES

Front

Strap

Bib

90 cm wide fabric

Size 8-10
Size 12-14
Size 16-18
GRAIN OF FABRIC

1 grid square = 5 cm / 2 in.

See instructions for sizes 16/18

Two-piece suit

Maternity Two-Piece

A two-piece suit for maternity wear can be extremely useful. It can be dressed up or dressed down for more or less any occasion. This dress was made up in coordinating grey and black check, with the top in silk crêpe-de-chine and the dress in wool/silk – an ideal combination for day or evening wear. You can choose from a selection, including Viyella, brushed cotton and lightweight wool. For evenings, wear this dress with high heeled shoes and a distinctive pair of earrings; use the cravat as a bow at the neck, or even tied in the hair. For daytime, wear it more casually, the shirt open and with the ties worn as a cravat or just loosely tied at the neck.

Size: to fit up to a size 14 (normal size) loosely. To make skirt larger, add width at side seams. To make top larger, slash pattern vertically on the grain line from mid-shoulder to hem and add width by spreading pattern pieces apart to suit. Actual finished length of skirt from waist 74cm/29in. Actual finished length of top 72cm/28½in.

Materials: 2.50m/2¾yds of 115cm/45in wide fabric for top and cravat.
1.70m/1⅞yds of 140 or 150cm/54 or 60in wide fabric for skirt.
30cm/⅜yd of two-way stretch jersey fabric any width for tummy panel.
1.10m/1¼yds of 2cm/¾in wide elastic for skirt.
9 12mm/½in buttons.
Lightweight Supershape Iron-On Vilene.
Pair of lightweight combination shoulder/sleevehead pads.
Matching thread.

Cutting out: follow the graph pattern to make a paper pattern using dressmakers' 5cm/2in squared pattern paper. Follow cutting layout to cut out skirt, top and cravat. Out of Vilene, cut out two collars and two front self-facings – see pattern.

Special note: it is possible to buy ready-made stretch maternity panels which you can substitute for the pattern piece we have supplied. These already include an elastic waistband section, so lay the panel 3cm/1¼in below upper edge of skirt front when fitting, and stretch it flat before pinning it in place –a good tip is to use the ironing board as a work table and pin through the padded top to keep the panel flat.

Follow the hints on sewing silk included in the christening robe pattern (see page 130) – other special making-up hints are included in the following instructions.

Seam allowances of 15mm/⅝in are included in the pattern.

Making up

Skirt: lay wrong side of stretch panel on top of right side of front, top edges even, matching centre fronts. Zig-zag around outer edge, or use a special stretch stitch if available. Trim away main fabric underneath stretch panel close up to stitching. Pin and stitch front to back at sides, starting 3cm/1¼in below upper edge on one side only: press open and press under remaining seam allowances at one side. Press under 3cm/1¼in on upper edge and top-stitch 2.5cm/1in from fold, thus forming an opening in one side seam to insert elastic. Slot elastic through waistband casing, overlapping ends by 1cm/⅜in and stitching securely: pull out 15cm/6in of elastic and fold in half, stitching every 2.5cm/1in from fold so that there are three lots of excess elastic to be let out as pregnancy advances. Push elastic back into casing. Turn up 2cm/¾in hem and stitch in place.

Top: fuse Vilene to wrong side of front self-facings. Fold self-facings to right side and stitch 2cm/¾in from lower edge: trim, turn to right side and press. Press self-facings along foldline on right side and tack upper edges together. Top-stitch close to edge, round lower edge and up other side of self-facing 4cm/1½in from edge.

Pin and stitch fronts to back at shoulders, right sides facing: stitch again 6mm/¼in inside first stitching, trim seam allowances close to second stitching and zig-zag together: press towards back. Fuse Vilene to wrong side of collars. Press neck edge seam allowance to wrong side on one collar, trim to 6mm/¼in. Pin and stitch both collars together around outer edges: trim seam allowances and corners, clip to dot at centre front and turn to right side, press. Stay-stitch neck edge of top by stitching 3mm/⅛in inside seamline using small stitches. Pin and stitch unfinished neck edge of collar to neck edge of top, right sides facing, clipping top to stay-stitching on curved sections where necessary. Trim seam allowances and press towards collar. Slip-stitch remaining collar neck edge over first seam. Top-stitch collar close to all edges.

Run two rows of gathering stitches 10mm/⅜in and 15mm/⅝in from sleevehead between notches and pin and stitch to armhole, right sides facing, matching sides, notches and shoulders. Stitch again 6mm/¼in inside first stitching and trim seam allowances close to second stitching. Zig-zag together and press towards sleeve.

Pin and stitch side and sleeve seams together, right sides facing, in one continuous movement: stitch again 6mm/¼in inside first stitching, trim seam allowances close to second stitching and zig-zag together: press towards back.

Press under 5mm/3/16in at lower edge and turn up a further 15mm/⅝in hem. Top-stitch close to first fold. Make sleeve hems in same way.

Make nine horizontal buttonholes in right front, with one in lower part of collar 15mm/⅝in above neck edge, the next one 8cm/3in below, followed by one 4cm/1½in below that, then another pair 8cm/3in below and 4cm/1½in apart, and so on. Sew buttons to left front to correspond.

Cover shoulder/sleevehead pads with scrap fabric and tack to armhole seam allowances and shoulder seam allowances.

To make cravat, narrowly hem all round.

See cutting out plan overleaf.

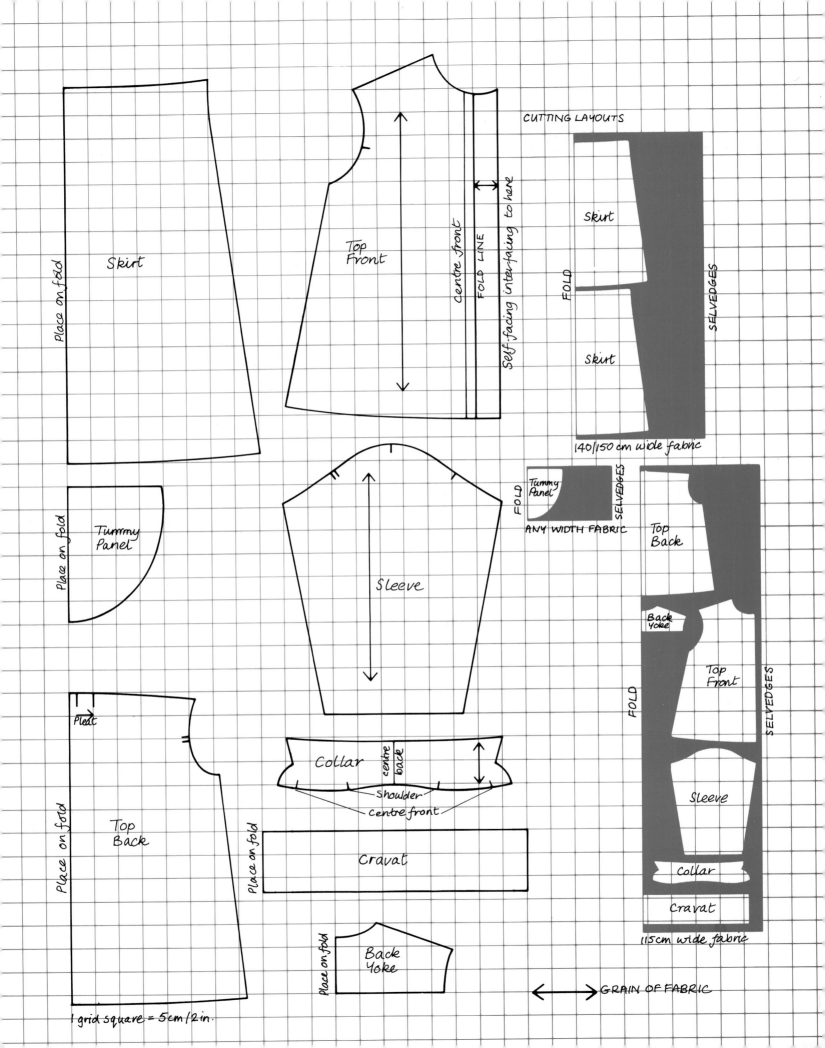

Skirt

Place on fold

Top
Front

centre front

FOLD LINE

Self-facing interfacing to here

Skirt

FOLD

Skirt

SELVEDGES

140/150 cm wide fabric

Tummy
Panel

Place on fold

Sleeve

Tummy
Panel

FOLD

SELVEDGES

ANY WIDTH FABRIC

Top
Back

Back
Yoke

FOLD

Top
Front

Pleat

Top
Back

Place on fold

Collar

centre back

shoulder

centre front

Cravat

Place on fold

Sleeve

SELVEDGES

Collar

Cravat

115cm wide fabric

Back
Yoke

Place on fold

⟷ GRAIN OF FABRIC

1 grid square = 5cm/2in.

Evening dress

Finally, here is the dress for that special occasion – a party, an evening at the theatre, or whatever: something for you to look stunning in. This drop-waist dress with a drawstring fastening is very simple (always the essence of stylish dressing) but extremely attractive. It needs to be made in a drapable fabric that isn't too stretchy (a fine jersey that has weight so that it is not too flimsy would work), and preferably in not too bold a pattern, as this tends to date rather quickly. A pattern with a self-spot or a plain fabric is better, as you can wear it with more things. Ours is made in silk crêpe-de-chine with a self-spot in silver grey with midnight blue trim.

Size: to fit up to a size 14 (normal size) very loosely

Materials: 4.40m/4⅞yds of 90cm/36in wide fabric.
1m/1⅛yds of 90cm/36in wide contrast fabric.
Lightweight Supershape Iron-On Vilene.
1.70m/1⅞yds of 2cm/¾in wide bias binding.
75cm/30in of 15mm/⅝in elastic.
Matching thread.

Cutting out: follow the graph pattern to make a paper pattern using dressmakers' 5cm/2in squared pattern paper. Follow cutting layout to cut out dress and contrast dickey and bow. Out of Vilene cut four collars, one front neck and one back neck facing. For ties, cut from main fabric two straight strips 50cm x 6cm/20in x 2⅜in.

Special note: follow the hints on sewing silk listed with the christening robe instructions (page 130). Silk crêpe de chine, which we used here, is a beautiful but tricky fabric to work with, and is really not suitable for tackling by any but the very experienced.

Seam allowances of 15mm/⅝in are included in the pattern.

Making up
Make buttonholes in front and back where marked, reinforcing on the wrong side beforehand with a square of Vilene.
Pin and stitch front to back at shoulders, right sides facing: trim seam allowances to 6mm/¼in and zig-zag together, press towards back.
Fuse Vilene to wrong side of collars, front neck and back neck facings. Right sides facing, pin and stitch two collars together round all edges except neck edge: trim seam allowances and corners and turn to right side, press. Tack neck edges together. Assemble remaining two collars in the same way. Pin and tack the two finished collars to neck edge of dress, with wrong side of collars to right side of dress, matching centre backs, shoulders and lower +.
Right sides facing, pin and stitch front neck facing to back neck facing at shoulders and press seams open. Pin and stitch facing to neck edge of dress, right sides facing, matching shoulders and lower Vs. Reinforce lower V by stitching again over first stitching and slash to point. Trim seam allowances and press facing to wrong side. Understitch facing by stitching close to seam on right side through all thicknesses using small stitches – this will help prevent facing from rolling out. Tack facing down at shoulder seams. Fold dickey in half along foldline, wrong side inside, and tack round edges. Pin to lower edges of front neck facing matching centre fronts: stitch round outer edges. Open out collars and stitch along original neck seamline through dickey. Pin and stitch sleeve to armhole, right sides facing, matching notches and shoulders: stitch again 6mm/¼in inside first stitching, trim seam allowances close to second stitching and zig-zag together. Press seam allowances towards sleeve.
Pin and stitch side and sleeve seams together in one continuous movement, right sides facing. Trim seam allowances to 6mm/¼in and zig-zag together: press towards back.
On wrong side, pin and stitch bias binding centrally over casing line, starting at a side seam and turning under ends where they meet: slip-stitch ends together. Fold tie ends in half lengthwise, right side inside, and stitch along long edge and one short edge. Trim seam allowances and corners, turn to right side: press. Lap unfinished ends 15mm/⅝in over ends of elastic and stitch securely. Slot through casing through buttonholes so that tie ends only extend.
Turn under 15mm/⅝in sleeve hems and press: stitch in place. Turn under 15mm/⅝in dress hem and press: stitch in place.
Fold bow in half lengthwise, right side inside, and stitch round outer edges, leaving a gap at centre point to turn. Trim seam allowances and corners and turn to right side: press and slip-stitch gap together. Gather bow along centre line and pull up: stitch to centre of dress just below dickey and tie in a bow.

142

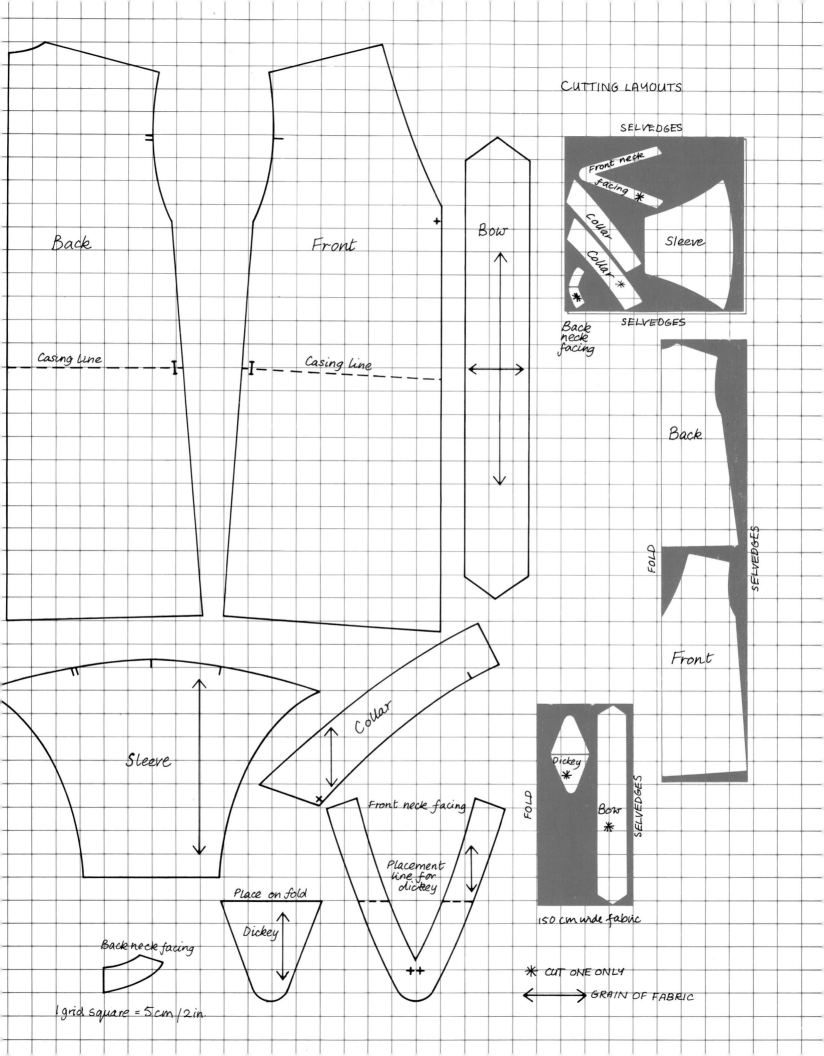

Back

Front

Bow

Casing Line

Casing Line

Sleeve

Collar

Front neck facing

Placement line for dickey

Place on fold

Dickey

Back neck facing

1 grid square = 5cm / 2 in.

CUTTING LAYOUTS

SELVEDGES

Front neck facing

Collar

Collar

Sleeve

Back neck facing

SELVEDGES

Back

FOLD

SELVEDGES

Front

FOLD

Dickey

Bow

SELVEDGES

150 cm wide fabric

✳ CUT ONE ONLY

⟷ GRAIN OF FABRIC

Useful Addresses

Dancercise
Dancercise, The Barge Durban, Lion Wharf, Richmond Road, Old Isleworth, Middlesex. Classes all over Greater London and Surrey; also at companies and schools by arrangement. See also *Dancercise* by Phyllis Greene Morgan (*Methuen, London 1983*).

David Hicks
David Hicks International, 101 Jermyn Street, London SW1. (Main design Office).

David Sassoon
Bellville Sassoon, 73 Pavillion Road, London SW1.

Designers Guild
Designers Guild products are available world-wide. For information on specific countries please contact: Designers Guild London Office, 277 King's Road, London SW3 5EN.

Dragons
Dragons of Walton Street, 23 Walton Street, London SW3 2HX.
Dragons of Brighton, 6 Prince Albert Street, Brighton, Sussex.
See also *Rooms To Grow Up In (Ebury Press, London 1984)*.

Jan Vanvelden
36 Lexington Street, London W1.

Laura Ashley
Laura Ashley Ltd, Carno, Powys, Wales. (U.K. Head Office).
Europe: (Head Office)
Laura Ashley Manuf. B.V., PB 1288, 5700 AC Helmond, Netherlands.
U.S.A. (Head Office)
Laura Ashley Inc., 714 Madison Avenue, New York 10021.
Canada: (Head Office)
Laura Ashley, 4800 Jean Talon Street West, Montreal, Quebec H4P 2M7.
Australia: (Head Office)
Laura Ashley, 17-23 Queensbridge Street, South Melbourne, Victoria.

Linda Beard
Linda Beard, Coloroll, Crawford Street, Nelson, Lancashire.

Patons.
Patons & Baldwins Ltd, Alloa, Clackmannanshire, Scotland.

Australia:
Coats & Patons Australia Ltd, 321-355 Fern Tree Gully Road, P.O. Box 110, Mount Waverley, Victoria 3149.
U.S.A.
Susan Bates Incorporated, 212 Middlesex Avenue, Route 9A, Chester, Connecticut 06412 .
Canada:
Patons & Baldwins (Canada Ltd), 1001 Roselawn Avenue, Toronto.
South Africa:
Mr Bob Theis, Marketing Manager, Patons & Baldwins (South Africa) Pty, P.O. Box 33, Randfontein 1760.

Viyella
Viyella House, Somercotes, Derby DE55 4JN.
U.S.A.
Richard Brooks Fabrics, 125 Inwood Village, Dallas, Texas.
    Maxine Fabrics, 417 Fifth Avenue, New York.
    Sew Magnifique, 3220 Paces Ferry Place N.W., Atlanta, Georgia.
    Britex Fabrics, 146 Geary Street, San Francisco, California.
Australia:
Fletcher Jones & Staff Pty, P.O. Box 100, Warrnambool, Victoria 3280.
    David Jones Pty Ltd, P.O. Box 503, Sydney, N.S.W. 2001.
    Georges Ltd, P.O. Box 765G, 162 Collins Street, Melbourne, Victoria 3001.
Henry Buck Ltd, 320 Collins Street, Melbourne, Victoria 3000.
South Africa:
Garlics, Group Buying Office, P.O. Box 63, Adderley Street, Cape Town.
    James McDonald's Wynberg Stores, P.O. Box 123, Wynberg, Cape Province.

Warm & Wonderful
Warm & Wonderful, 191 St John's Hill, London SW11.

Picture credits

Reproduced by Gracious Permission of Her Majesty the Queen: 43, 46 (both), 52 (top), 68 (top left), 79 (top left), 97 (top left, below left), 99 (below left), 100 (top), 103 (top).

Tim Graham: pages 7, 8, 11 (both), 12, 13, 14 (all three), 15, 16 (all three), 18, 19, 20, 21, 26, 27, 29, 41, 42, 44, 45, 50, 51 (top right), 52 (below, left and right), 54, 55, 59, 61 (below, left and right), 65, 66 (below left), 69 (below right), 72, 76, 102 (top left).

BBC Hulton Picture Library: page 101 (top).

Camera Press: pages 22, 47 (below left), 48 (top left), 58 (top left), 102 (below).

David Hicks: page 81.

Designers Guild: pages 93-95.

Illustrated London News: pages 47 (top left), 56 (top right), 67 (top), 70 (below), 99 (top).

Heywood and Martin/Chris Welch: pages 109, 111, 114, 115, 118, 121, 124, 127, 128, 131, 134, 137, 140, 143.

Jane Tyrrell: pages 107, 110, 112, 116, 119, 122, 125, 129, 132, 135, 138, 141.

John Scott: pages 49 (top), 58 (top right and below), page 63 (below right), 64 (top left and right, below left), 66 (below right), 100 (below), 101 (below left).

John Topham: pages 48 (top right), 62, 63 (below left), 66 (top), 67 (below left), 68 (top right), 79 (top right), 97 (below right), 101 (below right).

Keystone: pages 25, 49 (below left), 60, 63 (top), 67 (below right).

Laura Ashley: pages 83, 84-85.

Linda Beard: pages 90-91.

Mary Evans Picture Library: page 51 (top left).

Mothercare: page 80.

Paul Press: pages 86-89.

Photographers International: pages 59 (top left and below right), 64 (below right).

Phyllis Greene Morgan/Bridget Morley: pages 31-39.

Popperfoto: pages 69 (left, top right), 70 (top), 71 (all three), 72 (top, right and left), 99 (below right), 103 (below).

Press Association: pages 53 (top right), 98 (top left).

Rex Features: pages 56 (top left), 61 (centre right), 98 (top right), 102 (top right).

Syndication International: pages 53 (top left), 61 (top right), 73 (below).

Time Life: page 57.

PRINTED IN BELGIUM BY proost INTERNATIONAL BOOK PRODUCTION